Sex Free

A (not so) Modern Approach to Dating and Relationships

Monique N. Matthews

Sex Free:
A (not so) Modern Approach to Dating and Relationships

Copyright © 2012 Monique N. Matthews

Book design by Afiya Owens-Khalfani

ISBN-13: 978-0615674254
ISBN-10: 0615674259

Photographs by Greg Worsham, Lifestyles Photography

For Grandma,

Gladys L. Mickey

I'd do anything for you, again and again, because you did everything for me.

CONTENTS

INTRODUCTION

As the name suggests, someone who is sex free is choosing, for one reason or another, to refrain from sexual intercourse. Fundamental to this definition is the word choice. This is why being sex free is not the same as not being able to "get any."

If one is unable to "get any," it generally means that due to some type of lack in his or her life – money, home, job and/or pleasant personality – others do not find him or her desirable. A person who can't get any does not ever need to tell anyone that he or she has trouble in this area. His or her inability to attract a suitor is plainly visible to all in sight.

If you find yourself in this demographic, then sadly this book is not for you.

Sex Free: A (not so) Modern Approach to Dating and Relationships is for those individuals who willingly choose, for one (or a series) of reason(s), to opt out of having sex for a period of time. The timing is generally relative to their goal, and after they achieve it, they re-enter the world of physical intimacy refreshed, renewed and ready to take their lives and relationships to the next level. There are many reasons to take a sex-free sabbatical, as we will discuss in the book. But, never, at any point during your journey, should an absolute stranger be able to gaze upon you and know that you aren't "getting any." For, as you will see, not only is your sexuality your business, becoming sex free should make you sexier.

Yup, you read me right: *Becoming sex free should make you sexier.*

Before you toss this book to the side and think I'm crazy, consider this: only someone who already owns his/her sexiness or sex appeal could even consider becoming sex free. *Hence, sexier.*

Additionally, humans have a tendency to want what we cannot have. We are drawn to others who are confident, open, loving, smart and physically attractive. We like people with goals, who are focused, who not only know what they want, but also pursue it. We also admire those who don't easily bend to pressure or let circumstances keep them down. And, all these traits are apparent or further developed in anyone choosing to be sex free in today's world.

Real Talk:

Our world is oversaturated with sex. Everyone seems to be doing it, as often as they'd like and with as many partners as they can muster up. Yet, few people seem to find the longstanding happiness our music, television programs, and films suggest we should derive from having it. Even fewer are living the lives of their dreams with purpose, passion, and genuine love. Perhaps that is because we are distracted by what society is telling us will make us happy and not spending enough time with ourselves to find out what will really make us happy.

2

I do not pretend to have all the answers. I certainly would never offer myself as a poster child for abstinence, though at the time of publication, I have been sex free for over seven years. My motivation, as I'm sure the same will be true for yours if you decide to embark on this journey, was very personal to me. I wanted to achieve my goal more than anything else, which made my choice to say no to sex much easier. That does not mean, however, that I will never have sex again. Nor does it mean that with the exception of revealing how long I've been sex free in this book that I will publicly discuss it again.

I also believe that sex is sacred. I realize that in our society we can talk about and treat sex as if it is as common as a game of flag football on a lovely Sunday morning or a casual night of dancing at the hottest club. And while sex can be fun, intoxicating, and exciting, it is also a very special way to express deep affection for another human being. Thus, I fundamentally believe that one's choice to be sex free for as long as he or she chooses is no one's business but that person's.

I offer an approach. If you've picked up this book, it is not by accident. You have been drawn, for one reason or another, to the idea of becoming sex free. I know that when I began my journey I had an extremely hard time finding any resources for how to do it. What I did find was often laced with a strict judgmental tint that often amounted to advice advocating that the only way to do it was to withdraw from the world. Yet, I love people and life. I also didn't believe

3

that my decision to become sex free should exclude me from being me – someone who likes going out, having fun, meeting new people, enjoying new experiences, and deepening the connection and closeness I may feel for a man I am strongly attracted to.

The good news is that I found that not only did I not have to abandon myself; I have actually become more of myself. I am more open, outwardly loving, and kind than I can ever remember being as an adult. Like many of you, I, too, have had some life and relationship experiences that shook me to my core. There were times when I wondered if I would ever love again. And then, when I least expected it, because I was so busy focusing on staying true to being sex free, I found the childlike wonder and hope for new possibilities that my adulthood self assured me was too good to be true. Hence, it is in this spirit that I submit *Sex Free: A (not so) Modern Approach to Dating and Relationships* to you. May it provide you with some guidelines, inspiration and support during your own, very personal journey.

Welcome… your sex-free journey awaits!

WHAT EXACTLY IS SEX?

It may seem weird to include a chapter questioning the meaning of sex. However, when you consider the first definition listed in Merriam-Webster, "sexually motivated phenomena or behavior," you'll find the meaning is rather vague. After all, what exactly falls under the category of phenomena and/or behavior?

Most heterosexuals, for instance, would classify sex as the penetration of the vagina by the penis. Indeed, Merriam-Webster confirms this definition via its second meaning, listed as sexual intercourse or coitus. However, it also includes, "intercourse (as anal or oral intercourse) that does not involve penetration of the vagina by the penis."

And, it is this definition of oral sex as indeed sex that may give one pause. See, even though oral sex involves the usage of male and female genitalia, most people do not see it as sex *exactly*.

After all, our very own former President Bill Clinton vehemently denied having sexual relations with White House intern Monica Lewinsky in the oval office. And, when the truth emerged that she did, in fact, give him a blow job, and that he did, in fact, penetrate her with an external object (i.e.: a cigar), Clinton became the first sitting president in the United States to be impeached for lying under oath.

During President Clinton's trial and subsequent judgment, scores of conversations could be heard around the country questioning whether or not he actually lied. While Merriam-Webster, for example, would note that according to its definition, he did lie, the Oxford Dictionary would most likely speak up for the former president, insisting that he did not, as its lexicon includes no such appendage for oral and/or anal sex in its discussion of sexual intercourse.

So, when I decided to become sex free, I found myself flooded with questions, both by close friends and colleagues I confided in and within myself, about what really constitutes a sex-free lifestyle. In turn, I decided to consult one of my friends who had publically declared herself to be sex free for years prior to my decision.

Over tiramisu and latte's, I asked Connie[1], "Is oral sex, sex?"

"It isn't to me," said Connie, a self-professed Christian, who adopted a sex-free lifestyle as part of her faith, while she nonchalantly sipped her caramel macchiato.

I thought about how so many pastors I knew would insist that not only was oral sex forbidden, they would also consider it a vile and disgusting example of "sexual immorality."

---

[1] A few of the names included in the examples have been changed to protect an individual's privacy.

Then, Connie reminded me that the term "sexual immorality" is vague and subject to interpretation. See, Connie believes that a great deal of the religious leaders who are highly critical of oral sex are "old school," and as such reflect the social mores specific to the time period in which they were raised.

And, just like that: *Bam!* I was, once again, presented with another "vague" term in reference to sex that was open to interpretation.

I began turning inward, by taking a long, hard look within and asking myself the following questions:

- Short of physical penetration, if I were to partake in any physical pleasure, oral or otherwise, would it be easier for me to get caught up "in the moment" and forgo my commitment to abstinence? In other words, how far was safe enough to go before I gave in to temptation?

- Given that not only are men are physical beings who are used to physical contact, but also that this it is relatively easy for a man seek physical pleasure from someone else, can I honestly expect a man to want to spend time with me if I'm not pleasing him in a physical way?

- How would I feel after I partook as a recipient or a giver of any oral or physical-based pleasure, especially if my partner was not someone I was (or could become) serious about?

- If I removed all types of sexually stimulated pleasure from the equation, how could I determine the difference between a platonic friend and a "boyfriend?"

The answers didn't come quick. They evolved over time. After more and more self-reflection on my end. One of the things I realized early on is that I did not want to place myself in a position to fall. Anything can happen in the heat of the moment. In the best-case "fail" scenario, I could forego my sex-free status because the physical stimulation from receiving head was so good that I didn't care what happened beyond that moment.

In a mediocre outcome, I could open myself to a physical experience with a man and have it be less than fulfilling. And, if it wasn't good, because let's keep it real, everyone doesn't know how to "go downtown," I'd be mad.

Finally, in the worst case scenario, I could place myself in a most vulnerable position where even if I said no, my partner could determine that my no meant yes, or that I was in some way teasing him, and proceed to enter my body anyway. Date rape, or acquaintance rape, is real, especially as a recent Department of Justice report reveals that somewhere in America a woman is raped every two minutes.[2] Nearly 70%

---

[2] U.S. Department of Justice. *National Crime Victimization Survey.* 2006-2010.

of women raped know their attacker. And, at least four out ten women are raped in their own home.

Then, I considered my other questions and how the majority of them were motivated by fear – fear of losing him, even a him that was yet to be mine, and I realized that I could lose him anyway. Even if I was having intercourse with a man, there's no guarantee that he wouldn't go outside of our arrangement to have sex with someone else, especially if he told me "from the gate" that he wasn't interested in being exclusive.

I even factored in one or two experiences we women love to file in the "never happened" category. You know those encounters where you wondered what the heck you were thinking and shuddered at the realization that you actually had sex with that guy.

Ultimately, I realized that one's reasons for choosing to undergo a sex-free journey provides the best definition in terms of whether one includes oral sex or any other physically stimulated pleasure as sex. For example, if someone commits to a sex-free lifestyle in obedience to his/her faith, than his/her holy text makes it very clear. The Bible, for instance, tells those who believe to abstain from all natural or physical pleasure to receive the promises of God. So, it's clear that if you choose to forgo sex outside of a marriage covenant, then all types of fleshly pleasure, including oral sex, are off limits.

If, however, you decide to become sex free for any other reason, then your decision to potentially practice oral sex, even while abstaining from physical penetration, is based largely on one's internal (moral) compass, level of discipline and will power. As you determine what exactly is sex, take the time to honestly access where you fall along the spectrum in regards to these aforementioned factors. Then, act accordingly. Remember the goal is to succeed. Hence, be wary of biting off more than you can chew. And, if you find that you have, reassess your beliefs and values to ensure that you place yourself in the best possible position to thrive in a sex-free lifestyle.

Fellas, in regards to our discussion about reasons why one may try to adopt a sex-free life style, we are going to start with you. Yes, you. And, do you know why? Because I know that just because many of you enjoy sex and are able, much more than your feminine counterparts, to see sex strictly as a physical release, similar to how one may go to the gym and lift weights or play a quick game of pick up basketball, there are times when you may consider that life might be a whole lot easier if your second head wasn't making the majority of decisions for you.

Plus, we live in a society that defines a large percentage of your manhood in terms of sexual conquest. Beginning as boys, you may have received the message very clearly that "you have to sow your oats." You may have also been told that having multiple conquests is simply something "that a man does," especially if you were raised in a single parent household where there were no men there whose physical presence alone may have been enough to counteract those claims or if you were raised in an unhappy two-parent household where other factors besides love, monogamy and commitment kept your parents together.

But, if you're reading this, chances are you are no longer a boy. You are a man— A clear thinking, strong-willed, independent spirit capable of making decisions apart from what others expect of you. You have enough life experience to know that you're in charge. You rule your body. It doesn't rule you. You are not some depraved animal without any ethics or integrity that lacks control of his body. Indeed, by this point, many of you have your code – of do's and don'ts, and when and won'ts – and that, more than anything else, determines where and with whom you choose to have sex.

Yes, I've listened. I've heard when you've confessed that sometimes you didn't even feel like having sex when your money wasn't right. A great deal of you take the societal role of provider very seriously, and when you're challenged in that area, you don't want to do anything besides figure out how to get a job, attain more security in your career, and/or brainstorm ways to build wealth, so you are never in such a financially vulnerable situation again.

Further, there are times when the purportedly most strong and virile among you, the professional athletes, especially boxers, swear off sex until a major goal is met, ala a big fight. Sex, as many a boxer's trainer will tell you, is not only a distraction, it makes men lose power. And these trainers don't want their prized gladiators to indulge, at least not, until the championship belt is won.

Most men, in some way, look at themselves as gladiators in pursuit of some goal. If you're one of these guys, relax and keep reading. This chapter was created and designed specifically for you.

And, ladies, if there are any disbelievers among you

12

who doubt whether or not men can purposely abstain for any length of time, I invite you to keep reading as well. Not only will you get the opportunity to learn more about our complementary cohort, you may also get a very clear idea of the very things that turn men off... and on.

Reason #1: Rule Your Own Ship

TV is chockfull of images of men putting their significant others off, especially during football season, when a game is on. The variations of the scenario may be different depending on whether it's part of a storyline in a sitcom or a commercial advertisement for pizza, beer, or the like. Yet, the message is always the same: there are times when a man will shun a woman's advances, in favor of something he wants more.

But, need those images only be on display during football season when mass media, in some form or fashion, is trying to sell you something by using the sexes against each other?

What about those times when you and your girl get to a place where you are really comfortable with one another? You come over and prefer to sit down on the sofa, chill and watch TV, but know that that would be a huge "no no."

Why? Because you've both heard the adage directed towards women, "If he's not getting it from you, he's getting it from somewhere else." So, while you're sitting there watching Shaq, Kenny, Barkley and EJ on TNT, Sunday Night Football or a movie, she's wondering whom you're screwing

13

on the side. Truthfully, you're just tired. But, do you say that? No, you indulge, performing when you don't really want to and secretly building up resentment that you can't just "chill."

So, consider ruling your own ship. Refuse to succumb to peer pressure. Have sex on your own terms, in your own way, when it's not just an activity others expect you to perform on cue.[3]

Reason #2: Go For Your Own Gold

Just as athletes are not the only ones to compete to win a prize, they are also not the only ones who set goals. Most men do. So, what determines the level of success one has in making, keeping and accomplishing his goal? That, my friends, comes down to one specific word: Focus.

If you want to succeed, you've got to eliminate distractions. It's nearly impossible for a man, any human in fact, to accomplish anything worthwhile when he's being bombarded by texts, calls, Facebook messages, tweets and the like. Multiply that by the amount of time it takes to persuade a woman to sleep with you, actually sleep with her, spend the mandatory cuddle time afterwards and replicate that by one, two, or however many more, and you have a distracted and

---

[3] If you are currently in an intimate relationship, it is probably best to have a discussion with your partner about your desire to rule your own ship. Communication and understanding are keys in any relationship. Hence, if your decision will affect someone else, please share your decision ahead of time to avoid any misunderstandings.

exhausted Johnny with little to no time left to dedicate to rising higher than his current pay-grade. Chances are that poor John-Boy, and most any other man in his circumstance, will never accomplish his dreams. And, if he does, he'll be so stressed in the pursuit of it, especially with all of the distractions, that he'll rarely enjoy it. Even worse, he'll have even less time to set and accomplish an even greater goal. Don't let this be you. Break from the herd. Run your race in such a way that you win the gold.

Reason #3: Honor Your Faith

Islam expressly forbids sex outside of marriage. So does Christianity. And, while the Torah does not expressly prohibit premarital sex, it does revere sex within marriage as a sanctified and holy act.

Hinduism celebrates sex as a tool for recreation, yet it also places emphasis on abstinence, or brahmachayra, as evidence of spiritual maturation. It is considered an incredibly useful tool in helping men harness the energy of the body, for one's semen (veeryn) is considered sacred. In Hinduism, men who restrict the releasing of semen, save for procreation, are purported to achieve enhanced intellectual and spiritual capabilities.

Hence, no matter your faith, if you adhere to the principles of one of the world's major religions, chances are that your spiritual walk will directly contradict your natural impulses to please the body. And, if so, this does not mean that you will stop having sex; it may mean, however, that you may experience guilt and condemnation as a result of going against your spiritual beliefs.

Yet, if you find yourself weary of tugging these ambiguous emotions around like excess baggage, becoming sex free may just be the ticket for you. There have been men, some very powerful and/or living very high profile lives, who used their faith as motivation to say no and live their lives, condemnation free.

Like you, these men understand that they live in a culture that deeply reveres men who have a lot of sex, and one that will also question a gentleman's manhood if he refuses to place his natural impulses over spiritual obedience.

Retired NBA standout, A.C. Green, for example, recalled countless stories in various magazines about his Los Angeles Laker teammates and friends challenging and questioning his decision to remain not only sex free, but also a virgin, until he married. And, when A.C., a Christian, refused to have sex prior to his marriage at age 38, many people, in addition to his teammates, thought he was crazy. They could not fathom a heterosexual man shunning the sexy, beautiful women that his teammates would often sneak into his room. Nor did many understand him choosing not to hang out at popular clubs when his team traveled in order to avoid temptation.

Perhaps you can consider A.C. a kindred spirit. Let go of the guilt and step into the strength that a sex-free life can bring.

In addition, focus on the blessings that you will reap as a reward for your obedience, such as increased confidence in your spiritual walk and ever expanding favor in all areas of your life. You also gain greater discernment and an improved ability to see beyond the physical. This may help you better choose which interactions will yield higher rewards, not only for you, but also for everyone involved.

Reason #4: You've Got to Pay to Play

Given the women's rights movement beginning in the late 1800s to early 1900s, the "Sex & The City" sexual enjoyment movement of the late nineties to early 2000s, and all the music of the last few decades promoting female power through using men as sexual objects, you'd think there might be some real and substantial changes in the dating game where men and women come to the table evenly, bond over perfectly good, no-strings attached sex, and amicably walk away when the deed is done.

But, no it hasn't happened. And, it won't, at least in this society. Men will always "pay to play." Courtship, even if it's sidelined into merely "hooking up" or "kicking it" will involve an exchange. You may not always take a woman out, but you will have to take her out sometimes. Or, even if you don't and you eat at home, at some point you'll have to pay the grocery bill for that meal, too. Everything adds up.

Additionally, the more women you try to hook up with, the more you'll be paying. At some point, several grown men that I've spoken with confess that they eventually hang up their player suits because it's no longer financially viable, especially in this economy.

Sometimes, the payment isn't always financial. Even in the best of scenarios where you and a partner mutually agree to an emotion and commitment free sexual relationship (prior to ever doing the deed), there will be complications. Emotions, whether you want them to or not, will develop on either or both sides. We are humans. We are hard-wired for connection. Accept and deal with it.

Make it your choice to pay when, where and with whom you want to play with. Decide to abstain to become more selective, which will help you not only build up your bank account and any chance for making wealth, it will also empower you to avoid many a grown man's Achilles' heel... the "crazy chick."

Reason #5: Avoid the Crazies

Pssst... come closer. I have a secret to share – All women, even, no, especially the most mousy, well-mannered ladies you know are prone to become that "crazy chick." It can happen at a moment's notice. At least to you. For us, she's been brewing for some time. It might be in her interactions with you. It might be some mistreatment she received in prior relationships or even what she saw growing up as a child, but piss her off, slight her in any way, purposefully or not, and she may just flip on that crazy switch. Then, you're left shell-shocked, not understanding what happened, but wishing like hell that you never met her and hope to never meet any of her kind in your future.

But, you will, as long as there's some miscommunication about what the time you spend together really means. Gentlemen, if you know this woman really likes you and wants you for more than a sexual relationship, do not allow self-denial to rule. Don't fool yourself with, "Well, I told her I didn't want to be in a relationship." She's not hearing you. She's thinking that all men say that until they meet the right woman, and she's determined to be that right woman. She's thinking that time (and her special brand of "cherry") will change things/you.

If you willingly decide to go forth and continue a sexual relationship with her, she will, at some point, flip on you. If you pull away, become distant or cold, you are automatically the "*sshole," the crazy chick's counterpart. The *sshole is like gasoline for her. Instead of dissuading her, he makes her fire burn farther and wilder.

Why? Because she's hurt. She's angry. Maybe at you. Maybe with the world. At this point, it doesn't matter because she's keying in on you. She feels as if she's shared the most intimate part of herself with you, her body, and you disregarded it as if it were nothing. Yes, there are some women who see sex as mere fun, but it's not the majority of us. Biologically speaking, when we orgasm (even from sub-par sex), oxytocin, a body hormone is released in our brain. So, even if we don't really like you, if you hit that perfect spot? Ka-pow! We are now attached.

Have you ever seen a woman attached to a man that she doesn't even like? It's not pretty. On top of the attachment is anger and frustration at herself and you. Not only does she not get how she's into you when she knows she doesn't even like you as a person, she's furious at her own behavior. And, unless she's incredibly evolved and/or has amazing self-discipline to contain this fury, she will make your life a living hell.

This is when it pays to take a moment and chill. If you're so busy trying to sleep with us, you'll never learn how we really work. And, unfortunately, you'll keep finding crazy chick after crazy chick until you conclude that we're all crazy. Not so. We may all become crazy chick, but there are triggers, which bring her out. She is not automatic.

What you need is discernment. You need time to study us, apart from sleeping with us. If you allow your second head to defer to the one on top of your body with two ears, you'll learn to listen more. You'll make better choices. You may even inspire the crazy chick's bizarro twin, the "divine helpmate."

Reason #6: Best Sex of Your Life

There are many things married men don't tell single

men. Great sex is one of them. I am neither a man nor married, but I listen, as I previously confessed. I remember a few years back watching ABC's *Nightline*. *CSI: New York* actor Hill Harper was being interviewed along with radio host and relationship guru Steve Harvey, and Hill turned to Steve and asked him, "Why don't married men tell us the truth about all the benefits of marriage?"

Somehow Hill had stumbled upon the secret: happily married men experience better sexual satisfaction than their single counterparts. They also enjoy many more benefits than their single or cohabitating brethren, but we'll table this discussion for a future time.

For now, let's talk about sex – that beautiful, mind-boggling activity with the endorphin high like none other. Popular culture asserts that single men are in the best position to get the most sex of anybody. They are free, unencumbered by any emotional, spiritual or mental ties, and thus are most available to have as much sex as they want.

In truth, they're not getting it nearly as much or as frequently as *happily* married men are. And, even if you find that rare player who's "killing it" on the daily, there's no way he's reaping as much satisfaction on a consistent basis as his blissfully betrothed brother, because he's also enduring more crazy chicks, thinner pockets, and is probably, for all the other reasons stated above, less satisfied with his life outside the bedroom.

And, inside the bedroom? It's highly doubtful he's getting the best sex he can get. Sex is a physical activity. We all know that. But, great sex means that it involves much, much more. Some may say that the best sex comes from a deep, spiritual connection; others believe it's mental; still others purport that strong emotions reign supreme. But, nearly all agree that fantastic, time-suspending sex does not exist without both parties putting their all into it.

And, quite frankly, guys, unless a woman feels safe with you, you will never get all that she has to offer. Heck, many women may not even know that they're not giving all they've got. One of my best friends, Shana, who recently married, for example, confessed to me, "I am giving Dave things that I didn't even know I had." Shana thought that sex was good before she and Dave married when they were living together in a committed, monogamous relationship, but after they said their "I do's," she realized that she held a lot back, without even knowing it.

What makes Shana's case noteworthy is that she has always been someone who sought to please her man. Unlike the rest of our close-knit crew, Shana never fell for that "independent woman" spiel. She kept a man. She has always been very deeply committed to catering to her man. So, when she says she wasn't giving everything, my heart goes out to men who are interacting with any woman who's smiled, thrown their hands up in the club, or blasted the Destiny Child's single woman's anthem of the same name in her car – that is, the rest of us.

22

True, these men may be happy with their bowls of various cherries and they might think that all cherries taste the same. The sad part, of course, is that they may never know how delicious the cherry may truly be. Instead, they go round and round, like in a merry go-round, experiencing:

A. The Poverty Cherry

The poverty cherry is, by far, the most popular bowl of cherries on the market. It really comes into fashion when a woman arrives in her mid-to-late 20s, is still unmarried, and may be torn between whether or not she ever wants to be. This young lady is looking around and is struck by a growing fear of scarcity. She is ruled by the belief that there aren't enough men to go around and reasons that she's got to have sex with you, if she wants to keep you around. She may or may not even like you, but she's motivated by the thought that if she doesn't give it to you, you're going to get it somewhere else.

The truism attached to her guiding motif is not as important as the reason she chooses to have sex with you. She's mostly doing it out of fear. You may not know it, at least not early on. That's partly because she responds so "nicely" to your overtures for casual sex, or she might even initiate it, leaving you thinking that she might be a keeper.

The sex, at least initially, might be good to really good. Over time, however, it's just a "saltine," to borrow from the classic Eddie Murphy metaphor for sex. One day, you may wake up, or even finish as she's still laying besides you, disappointed by the idea that what you are eating is very far from a "Ritz."

It may not be her fault. It may not be yours either. Her actions, however, are motivated by fear. She's concerned with lack. Thus, there is no way possible she can sustain giving you great sex.

In addition, you also have to be very careful with this cherry. See, behind this vulnerable lady's seemingly laisse-faire approach to sex, you have a potential volatile cocktail of a woman motivated by fear who has had sex with you before she was emotionally ready to share herself. Before you know it, you may find *sshole in a reluctant dance with crazy chick. Best of luck there!

B. Sympathy Cherry

Kin to the poverty cherry is the sympathy cherry. This cherry, we, women, reserve for guys who may have stuck around long enough. Perhaps you saw us through a recent breakup or series of disasters. We've noticed that you're still hanging around. We're also a little lonely, so we decide to "give you some."

Or, maybe we think you have a lot of potential, and we reason that with a little help (i.e.: us changing you into someone presentable), you may be "alright." In this case, we may extend the sympathy cherry.

Though warm, sweet and mildly addictive, sympathy cherry takes its root in pity. And, make no mistake about it: a woman who pities you will never respect you.

C. Boomerang Cherry

Beware. Beware of the boomerang cherry, my dear friend, most of all, because you may really like it. Like the Reggie Hudlin-directed classic film *Boomerang* starring Eddie Murphy, Halle Berry, and Martin Lawrence, the woman who doles out this cherry, much like Robin Given's character, may mentally think a lot like you. She may really enjoy sex or at least has the understanding that it's as essential to spending time with men as air is for breathing, so she gives it up and it's probably very good.

The boomerang cherry's danger is not in the frequency or the pleasure of sex fading; it's how you will feel after it's over.

(*Sssh!* Yes, I said *feel*. I listen, remember, and I know that there are many ways in which you are far more sensitive than we as women. I'll continue to keep your secret if you want me to, but I must impress upon you the importance of how much damage interacting with a woman who wields the boomerang cherry can bring you. She will mock your strengths, exploit your weaknesses, and leave you bleeding.)

The woman bearing this cherry has been hurt. She's probably still hurting somewhere, but has decided that it's easier to cut herself off from that pain. So, the moment you try to open up and get emotional, either during cuddling afterwards or seeking some type of emotional support in the future, she's going to cut you in more ways than one.

Even if you unleash *sshole as a protective cover, she will have him running naked down the street away from you. See, she expects *sshole to come out, so when he does, she has every weapon already at her disposal to punish him for every other time he may have whipped her when she was, most likely, her former self, crazy chick.

Reason #7: Build a Forevermore
If all the discussion over the drama reaped from cherries, or stress from reflection of how sex can affect you in so many ways outside the bedroom has you exhausted, relax.

We've discussed enough stress and strife. Our last and final reason to consider a sex-free lifestyle is linked to your best chance for living a long, healthy and prosperous life: Build a forevermore.

Perhaps a few of you are already at the place where you're strongly considering a mate or maybe you've thought about it, but you've seen and heard such negative things about marriage that you figure, "I'm better off single."

Guess what? You're not. Not only do happily married men have more sex and report greater sexual satisfaction than their single or cohabitating counterparts (yeah, turns out that even if you have live-in "cherry," studies confirm that the levels of trust needed are not there to have this woman give you all she's got without reservations), they excel in nearly every other area of life.

Married men, for instance, experience better health – physically, mentally and emotionally than their unwed brethren. They live longer and experience significantly higher levels of physical and emotional health. A 2002 report in the Journal of Health and Social Behavior found that divorced or separated persons experienced a mortality risk 50 percent higher than those who were married. The study also revealed that the mortality gap between blacks and whites narrowed when marital status was taken into account.[4]

Married men are also less likely to get into trouble. For instance, a recent U.S. Department of Justice report reveals that male victims of violent crime are nearly four times more likely to be single than married. Married men also report lower levels of drug and alcohol abuse.

Further, if it's financial advantage and stability you seek, a trip down the altar with your divine helpmate may be just what your financial planner might order. A 2005 study of U.S. Navy officers reported that married men receive higher performance ratings and faster promotions than singles. Additionally, controlling for other factors including educational attainment, compared with unmarried men,

---

[4] Stephanie A. Bond Huie, Robert A. Hummer, and Richard G. Rogers, "Individual and Contextual Risks of Death Among Race and Ethnic Groups in the United States," Journal of Health and Social Behavior, Vol. 43 (2002), pp. 359–381.

married men, on average, earned 20 to 22 percent more than other men.

Of course, it's ill advised to just "jump the broom" for the benefits alone. The divorce rate isn't hovering at nearly 40 percent for nothing. It is essential that you choose the *right* partner – someone who not only believes in you and your plans, but is also somebody you can rally behind as well. You want someone who'd not only "ride or die" for you, but one who will also be able to hold down the fort should that need arise; and one who you'd be willing to go to bat for time and time again because what you're building, the forevermore, is worth it.

"How do you find her?" you may wonder.

Well, the physical space is not nearly as important as the mental, emotional, and perhaps spiritual location where you need to be. Beyond the basics, i.e.: she should be attractive to you, possess good hygiene, and someone you like as a person, there are two factors that are essential to finding her.

- **Know your roadmap**
  Gentlemen, you must know what you want out of life. You have to have worked out a five, ten, and perhaps even twenty-year plan of what you want your life to look like. Of course, you should account for hiccups and other possible changes along the road, but without a general direction, you are like a ship without a rudder, sailing nowhere fast.

- **Choose the best traveling companion for the journey**
  It's not enough to choose someone you like. Not only is
  that too broad because reasons for liking others vary
  and may be far-reaching, it's a pitifully sad tool for
  discerning your divine helpmate.

Some men think that all women are alike. They think
that if we're nice, pretty, and are fairly decent at sex, they can
hit the exchange button, and Pop! Get another one. I once
had a friend in college. He was an All-American basketball
star for a top 20 Division I program. He seemed to fall in and
out of love every other day. Then, suddenly, one day, he
eloped, surprising most of us who penned him as a good-
hearted lothario. (See, he didn't seem to like hurting people's
feelings; he was just one of those restless guys who "kept it
moving" when something potentially better came along.)

Eight years later, he was paying alimony and
Skypeingevery afternoon to his two kids who were nearly
1000 miles away. I asked, "What made you propose to your
ex-wife?"

He confessed what I just shared: he thought we were all
the same. He felt like he was ready to be married and chose
the one he was dating. Big mistake! They did not share
similar life goals. She also did not like the fact that he was
very family centered and wanted to live close to his family in
Los Angeles. Once the sex began wearing thin, they learned
that they did not do an effective job of communicating, and

they both had huge egos which prevented them from reaching out to one another before infidelity followed infidelity, on both their ends, and divorce became inevitable.

Thus, when you are choosing the person you want to be with to accompany you on the highs and lows on this journey called life, find the woman who can not only see the life you'd like to have, make sure that she can also help you get and keep it.

Next, talk to her about her goals. Be careful because she may initially say what she thinks you want to hear, especially if she's ready to be a bride. But, be very clear: a bride and a wife are two different things. A bride is the star of a beautifully, produced, one-day only show.

A wife is a position. Like any job, you must interview wisely. Don't just listen to what she says; watch what she does. Notice where and how she spends her time. You must be as equally committed to her success as she is to yours, so make sure that she is making career and life choices that you can rally around as well.

Trust me, even if you think that there's a wide field, once you see relationships through these lenses, the field will narrow. This lovely lady will be easy to spot because she will be a mirror of you: two wholes uniting together to form one forevermore.

Recently, I had breakfast with one of my dearest college friends who, because of work and other life responsibilities, I don't often spend as much time with as I'd like.

"Mo, I'm thinking of getting my tubes tied." I looked up to find Jazzy, pouring syrup on her recently arrived waffles with fresh strawberries and cream. The comment had to come from her, as there was no one at the restaurant's table besides the two of us, but her nonchalant demeanor seemed to directly counter the statement I just heard.

The fork went limp in my hand. This was quite a way to start breakfast.

"What do you think?" she asked. But, by the dazed and confused expression on my face, she already knew.

"I think it's pretty drastic. That's major surgery," I finally mustered.

Upon further research, I realized that it didn't have to be. While some still undergo general anesthesia to have their fallopian tubes seared to prevent an embryo from developing in their uterus, a growing number of gynecologists perform the cutting of a woman's reproductive organs by inserting implants in an outpatient procedure, which lasts less than an hour. Thus, although tubal ligations are still considered a permanent method of birth control, they are no longer considered major surgery.

Still, I was having difficulty dealing with the fact that someone I care so deeply for was willing to rip apart her insides because her outside reality didn't look so bright. More specifically, Jazzy's career was peaking, but her love life was not. Jazzy also has a few health complications, which now prevent her from taking the pill, so she thought having her tubes tied was the most rational alternative.

"How about you just stop sleeping with men you don't like?" I asked.

She looked at me like I was crazy. Mind you, I did not suggest she stop sleeping with men period; just learn to eliminate the ones who she did not get along with *outside* the bedroom.

Yet, as Jazzy looked at me and I looked at her, we both knew the reality of being a single woman in the dating game – sex is, all too often, a prerequisite, not a reward.

Ladies, when did the rules change?

When we were in our teens and early 20s, we were told to wait for someone special. Now, it doesn't seem to matter if he's special or not, if he has a xy chromosome and is breathing, most of us are willing to make a play. We are encouraged to buy into the scarcity and/or poverty mentality that there isn't enough, and instead of believing we can find the man who's our perfect match, we just want a man. And, of course, I get statistics. I read them too. But, numbers don't tell the full story. For instance, even in the deepest economic recession, someone, somewhere, is prospering. Apply that philosophy to love, and you may be among those who thrive in this field as well.

But, instead of focusing on how we can be one of the ones who succeed in love and life, most of us allow the negative to overwhelm us. Then, driven by the fear of competition, such as vast amounts of single women and dwindling resources, or the shortage of available, heterosexual men, we give up too much of ourselves before most of us are ready to do so.

One way we do this is by having sex before we are *truly* ready. And, yes, I realize that we're all adults, so biologically speaking, we don't need permission from anybody to do "the do." I'm talking about the check in the gut that lets us know that we may not be adequately prepared emotionally, mentally and spiritually to let someone physically enter our bodies.

Some of us will say we do it because it's fun, we're stressed, and/or sex is a great release. And, it's true. Sex can be all of these things. There are also others of us, however, who'll be the first to admit that we often do "the do" because we are keenly aware of the adage that if he's not getting it from us, he's going to get it from somewhere else.

Truthfully, he may. But, he also may be getting it from somewhere else and you, simultaneously. So, your giving it up before you are really ready to isn't helping your intent of stopping him. However, it might prevent him from getting to know the real you, and not the one so obsessed by fear and lack, that you become "crazy chick" and go off on him when the relationship is not progressing in the way or as rapidly as you'd like.

Granted, there are a few of us who only want a good time. But, most of us want more.

If you are one of the ones who want more, beware of sacrificing your self-respect to get a piece of a man, because if you do, you will probably get just that – a piece of a man. Then, you will have to be weary of complaining and blame the male, though, truthfully, he never even claimed to be a man. You may also be forced to admit, after much pain and heartache, that you didn't really take the time to see if you really wanted him; you merely wanted someone.

Case in point: a friend of mine recently had dinner with a single doctor who relocated to Atlanta. Noting the supposedly high proportion of single women to men, rumored to be around 20:1, but statistically reported as 2:1, she asked him about his dating life. Surprisingly, he shared that he wasn't dating that much. He was, however, having a great deal of sex. "I don't even have to ask a woman out," he said. "Most come up to me. If we do go out, they pay for it or go Dutch before I pull out my wallet."

Most of the women don't expect a second, let alone, a third date. They offer themselves up for a good time and he readily accepts. What shocked him most, however, was the Atlanta strip clubs. "There are a lot more women in there than I expected," he said. Instead of men having to go find women, the women go where the guys are. Even more alarming, for him, was that when the men didn't pay quick enough attention, these women started paying to receive lap dances from the strippers to up the ante. In turn, they may have been successful with him and other men for that night, but nothing long-term. Interesting enough, this confirmed bachelor also shared that he wasn't opposed to settling down. Unfortunately, he had yet to encounter a woman who inspired him to desire a more substantial connection.

Thankfully, not all women are like this. Even so, we cannot let the inmates run the asylum. I don't care how slim the pickings may look. We have way more power in this dating game than we are giving ourselves credit for.

Consider, for example, how much men have done historically for women they treasure. Both Caesar and Mark Antony, for instance, sacrificed their power as heads of the Roman state (the reigning world power at that time) for Cleopatra's attention and favor. In addition, there's hardly a movie, myth or fable that does not contain some element of a man sacrificing his all to win the heart of a woman. Heck, are you aware that even the Bible records (in Genesis 6: 1 – 2) that we as women are so desirable that angels sacrificed their immortality to marry and   have children with us?!

We are powerful, Ladies. Let's own it. Stop letting the terms of dating in the 21st Century be driven by our fears of scarcity and lack. Take the time to really see yourself through the total lens and not the current state of dating. If you're willing to slow down, and draw further into yourself, you may really understand all you have to offer to the world. Taking a sex-free sabbatical, for whatever duration you decide, may allow you to upgrade to a renewed, recharged, more loving, beautiful, and alluring you. In case you're circling the field, but still find yourself on the fence, consider the following for being sex free:

Reason #1: Invest In You

When we have sex, we are physically allowing another being to penetrate our core. Unlike our heterosexual counterparts, whose sexual organ is external, ours is located inside of us. Hence, when we let someone within, we let that person enter the center of our being. We take in his physical, as well as spiritual, emotional and mental energy. If he's not right in any way, it can affects us for hours, days, months, or even longer. We may feel slightly off – sad, agitated, and/or even angry and not know why. This is because we've let another human being deposit his energy and any other person's energy he's slept (or may simultaneously be sleeping) with inside of us. If we are not aware of this, we may blame ourselves for feeling crappy without an idea of how to fix it.

If you take the time to invest in yourself, you'll be in a much better position to know what's your "stuff" versus someone else's. You'll also have a better idea of consciously understanding what types of deposits a potential paramour is bringing to you and decide whether or not you want to receive them.

And, as you become more conscious of what energy may belong to you and what may belong to someone else, you'll be able to focus in ways you choose, and not potentially have it dissipated by trying to sort through energy that doesn't belong to you. This will enable you to have laser beam focus. Whereas a light bulb emanates light in a general way, a laser beam emits rays that are focused, direct and incredibly powerful. Imagine what you can accomplish with that type of dynamism!

Reason #2: Become a Better You

If you had any extra-time, what would you like to accomplish? I mean an achievement that almost makes you giddy with excitement by simply thinking about it. Is it career related? Educationally-inspired? Or, does it bring out your daredevil qualities? Like skydiving, perhaps? Or maybe your aspiration is a personal goal, like running a marathon, finishing a triathlon or at least starting with a 5K walk/race?

Do you even know? If not, no worries. This is what a sex-free hiatus is for.

As women, we spend an enormous amount of time being caregivers for everyone else. And, while it's certainly great to be there for others, it's hard to consistently show up and meet someone else's needs when we don't even attend to our own. It's very similar to the instructions flight attendants give before we take off on airplane flights. In the event of an emergency, the first thing we are encouraged to do is put on our own oxygen masks before we try and assist anyone else. This is because we can't aid another before we help ourselves.

When I was a child, my dad bought me a book entitled *How to Be Your Own Best Friend* during one of our weekly father-daughter dates. I was around eleven at the time, so I had no idea what the concept, perfectly summed up in the title, meant. Admittedly, I also thought the title, and hence concept, sounded stupid as most adolescent girls, including myself, relish fitting in. Yet, each year I am reminded how invaluable it is to treat, encourage, and love myself as deeply and kindly as I would my own best friend.

Becoming your own best friend is perhaps one of the best ways to become a better you because it can allow you to put yourself and your needs first without feeling as if you are being selfish. You are also training others how to treat you. If you don't take time to complete a goal and/or honor a personal desire or wish, others will feel that it's okay for them to ignore things that are important to you as well. They won't pay extra special attention to the things that matter to you, nor will they feel obliged to do so.

But, if you honor yourself by protecting, pursuing, and ultimately fulfilling those things that are special to you, then everyone who enters your life already has a working blueprint for interacting with you.

Taking the concept one step further, without becoming a better you, it may become impossible to get the best life has to offer. You may amass many things and become materially very successful, but you may also be plagued with a deep emotional void and emptiness you're not able to understand. This may result because you've done everything that "should" make you happy, but you haven't done the work to really locate what brings you pure, unadulterated joy.

For example, there are several popular relationship-improvement books, written by men, which tell women how men think. And, while it's great to have as many weapons in your armor to succeed in matters of the heart, it's at least equally important to know what it is that you want before you figure out how to think like a man or realize that he's just not that into you. Because, guess what? After a little soul searching during this "hiatus for self" time, you may realize that you were never into him either.

Reason #3: Enhanced Health

Since adolescence, most, if not all of us, have been warned of the life altering risks of an unplanned pregnancy and harmful, sometimes fatal, results of contracting a sexually transmitted infection. Hence, it's a no-brainer that the only way to prevent herpes, gonorrhea, HIV, and the like is to abstain. Most of us are also very well educated that a second option is safer sex where we use condoms. Less known, however, are the rising reports over the last decade about the growing risk of cancer, especially cervical and oral, associated with sex, that even condoms cannot prevent.

The human papillomavirus or HPV is a sexually transmitted infection that both men and women can get. It is spread via skin-to-skin contact and not by bodily fluids. Hence, condom use cannot stop the spread of this disease.

According to a 2011 Centers for Disease Control (CDC) report, approximately 20 million Americans currently have HPV, with six million new infections being discovered each year.[5] Additionally, nearly 80% of all sexually active women will contract HPV at some point in their lives. HPV can also lie dormant for many years, making it incredibly difficult, for some, to know who gave it to them. And, very often, men and women, alike, are unaware that they have it because not everyone who's infected has symptoms. Routine pap smears, which check for changes in cells on the cervix, are used to detect the disease in women. Unfortunately, there are no current detection methods for men. In addition, an increasing amount of dentists are beginning to routinely screen patients from oral sexual encounters during dental checkups.

---

[5] Centers for Disease Control (CDC). "Genital HPV Infection – Fact Sheet." 2011.

When symptoms do exist, they can take the form of warts on the genital area or lesions, bumps and skin discoloration in the throat, tongue or other areas within the mouth.

Most of the time, thankfully, the disease disappears by itself (i.e.: without any medical treatment) within two years. But, in those instances when it doesn't, HPV is the primary cause in all cases of cervical cancer for woman and now accounts for nearly 25% of all oral cancers.

Who would've thought that cancer would be the latest in a long string of health risks associated with sex? It's absolutely incredible. So, as you weigh your options for each possible sexual liaison, ask yourself, "Are the risks worth it to have sex with this person right now?" "Is he/she worth my life and/or quality of living?"

Your answers to these questions may provide much needed insight into your feelings for your prospective partner and the long-term possibilities for the relationship. They may also shed light on where you are mentally and emotionally, which can be another reason to embark on a sex-free hiatus.

In addition to increased physical health, becoming sex free can significantly contribute to increased mental and emotional health. Mental health can be defined as one's level of thinking, feeling and relating to others. A person suffering attacks to his/her mental health may experience depression, anxiety, and substance-abuse addiction, which may naturally affect her level of interaction with others. The quality of one's emotional health, which includes moods and the way an individual reactions to situations, also has a significant impact on how one deals with others. For example, if a person has unresolved anger issues towards someone in her past, these issues may manifest unexpectedly, at the most inappropriate time, threatening a current or future relationship.

In truth, all of us have experienced hurt and disappointment. So, it's not a question of whether or not we ever have a mental or emotional attack, it's a question about what we do *when* it happens.

Much like rest allows the physical body to recover when it's attacked by an ailment, a relationship respite, every now and again, can help us recover from wounding experiences. To illustrate, think about what happens when we experience symptoms signaling the beginning of a cold. If we immediately up our intake of vitamin C and zinc tabs, drink more liquids and rest, we diminish the length and severity of the cold. We also reduce the opportunity for us to infect others. But, if we don't take heed, or, even worse, do the opposite by continuing to eat poorly and not getting enough sleep, we are not only heading for a temporary shut down, where we can't get out of bed and/or move because our system is wore down, we can also make others sick in the process.

The same is true for our emotional health. When you are hurting, it's best to stop, rest and reflect, so that you can become renewed, refreshed and ready for whatever comes next.

Reason #4: Honor Your Faith

It's rare, if not impossible, to find major religions in the Western world that do not attempt to dissuade, if not outright demand that their believers refrain from, sex outside of marriage. If one looks closely, she will find that the reason is not because sex is vile or disgusting. The Bible, Torah, and Quran all regard sex as pleasurable, beneficial and even downright holy within the context of marriage. This is because the sharing of bodies often accompanies the exchange of mental, emotional and spiritual energy.

Within a covenant setting where two individuals agree, through good times and bad, to commit to one another, this exchange serves to strengthen their bond. If, however, the individuals are under no such agreement, the vulnerabilities each is exposed to can lead to massive dissension and destruction, on a personal and public level.

Unfortunately, as children, most of us who were raised with some type of religious background were mostly taught that sex was an egregious sin, which should be avoided at all costs. A great percentage of our elders did their best to persuade us to refrain from doing it by labeling it as dirty.

While this did not make most of us refrain when we came of age, it has resulted in a great deal of people carrying a huge amount of guilt, shame, and feelings of inadequacy. It has also resulted in quite a few believers still being unable to enjoy sex even within a covenant setting.

If you have ever felt (or currently feel) convicted in your spiritual walk because you have fallen short in this department, you well know condemnation is not enough to stop you from having sex. So, let it go.

Focus, instead, on the benefits.

Like those who practice Hinduism or Buddhism have heard that being sex free should not be used as a way to punish oneself, but as a way that one can reach greater spiritual, intellectual and emotional awakening, consider the many benefits your faith has for those who obey its holy writ.

Christianity, for example, is resplendent with benefits for obedient believers. The Word assures that if one comes boldly to the throne in a time of need, he or she will receive mercy (compassion, easing of distress) and grace (blessing, honor and favor). The main thing that can short circuit one's prayer from being answered is his or her ability to come boldly. Consider becoming sex free as a way to eliminate anything that will hinder you from receiving all the rewards God offers those who practice obedience.

Reason #5: Better Intimate Relationships

There once was a girl who recently graduated college and bought a plane ticket to move to a big city of lights where she thought her deepest desires might manifest. While checking her bags, she asked the ticketing agent if his job exposed him to a lot of people who lived in that city. The ticket agent said that he had. She then asked him what the people were like.

"What are the people like where you're from?" He asked.

"Oh, they're a mess." She started. "They say they're going to do things, but don't follow through. They talk really bad about you because they're very jealous. They are really afraid of someone else's success."

The ticket agent looked at her sympathetically, "I wish I could tell you different, but the people who live in the city you desire to go to are just like the ones you already know."

Dejected, the young lady asked him if he could book her a ticket to another city, a little less crowded and of a slower pace. He obliged. A short while later, another college grad approached this same ticket counter about going to the same big city of lights. Similar to his approach with the other young lady, the ticket agent also asked her about her experience with the city she was leaving.

"It was really fun," the hopeful graduate replied. "People were really kind and friendly. Everything wasn't always perfect, but no matter how bad it got, people found a way to smile and comfort one another until brighter days appeared.

Intrigued, he asked her why she'd leave, if she liked it so much.

"My time there was really great, but I graduated, which is what I came for. It's time to go because I believe life holds more for me."

She, then, looked intently at the ticket agent. Suddenly nervous about the city where she was traveling, "How are the people there? Do you think we'll get along?" The agent looked at her, and then broke into a warm, delightful smile. "They are a lot like the people you already know. You'll fit in quite well."

The preceding tale, and its many variations, which was first birthed as an African parable centuries ago, has endured because of its fundamental truth: wherever we go, we bring who we are.

Identify Your "Ish"

Granted, there are definitely times when we encounter situations and people that seem to come out of left field, but if you keep coming across the same type of person and/or experiencing the same type of issues in intimate relationships, it might be time to take a deeper look at the person in the mirror. Thus, your "ish" is the nonsense, mess or waste (as the term did derive as a polite way to avoid the four letter profane word for excrement) we have in our lives which stinks so bad that it threatens to prevent us from obtaining healthy relationships.

So, before you continue reading, please click on the link above or turn to the appendix to access the quiz.

Identify Your "Ish" Quiz

1. My life won't be complete until I am married.

    a. true

    b. false

    c. provided I have the wedding of my dreams

2. During my childhood, I was surrounded with adults who were happily married.

    a. true

    b. false

    c. occasionally

3. Sex is one of God's best gifts to mankind.

    a. true

    b. false

    c. that's hilarious

4. If a man takes me out to dinner, he is generally satisfied

    a. with the pleasure of my company

    b. if we have sex

    c. with whatever he gets

5. Men can never be faithful in a long-term relationship. At some point, he will cheat.

    a. true

b. false

c. depends on the man and/or circumstance

6. Intimate relationships are a distraction from my goals in life.

   a. true

   b. false

   c. depends on the partner

7. I experience orgasms during sex.

   a. often

   b. never

   c. rarely

8. I am ready to give my all to a relationship.

   a. true

   b. false

   c. as long as it won't fail

9. The majority of my friends are happily married.

   a. true

   b. false

   c. Ha! You've got jokes!

10. Having a man in my life is

   a. a distraction.

   b. normal.

   c. a fantasy.

11. Men love to be around me for the pleasure of my company.

    a. true

    b. false

    c. sometimes

12. I am one of the most fascinating and interesting people I know.

    a. true

    b. false

    c. to a small, select few

13. Men who I have been involved with have cried in my presence.

    a. true

    b. false

    c. not if he wants to get "pimp-slapped."

14. Men as well as women can easily have sex without getting attached.

    a. true

    b. false

    c. Absolutely

15. The man of my dreams

    a. does not exist

    b. will find me shortly

    c. is with someone else

Answer Key:
Please award yourself the following points based on your responses:

1.	2	1	3
2.	1	3	2
3.	1	2	3
4.	1	2	3
5.	3	1	2
6.	3	1	2
7.	1	3	2
8.	1	2	3
9.	1	2	3
10.	2	1	3
11.	1	3	2
12.	1	3	2
13.	1	2	3
14.	2	1	3
15.	2	1	3

     This quiz was created to help you access your views in three primary areas that affect the quality of our intimate relationships, namely our perceived self-value/worth, longstanding and current views on relationships, and attitudes towards sex. Scores range from 15 – 45 points.

If you score between 15 – 22 points:

You have your "ish" or issues under control. Whether or not you were exposed to a great deal of healthy, monogamous relationships growing up, you have a clear idea of not only what they look like, but also what you look like in one. You demonstrate a healthy self-worth by realizing that the value of your company is enough for any man, yet you understand that sex is a beautiful way to express strong feelings that two individuals may have for one another.

If you score between 23 – 33 points:

You still believe in a brighter tomorrow and the possibility of finding your ideal partner, however, you may have also seen and been through a few things, which have dampened your outlook. The upside is that you have many talents and gifts. There is only one you. Still, you may have had some encounters that left you wounded. As such, you may still be dealing with hurt, pain and disappointment. Some "me" time might be just what your internal doctor would order to facilitate your healing.

If you score between 34 and 45 points:

You may want to ease up on any Facebook postings about relationships or going out to a club, lounge, or the like to meet a man for a while. Chances are your Facebook friends, with the exception of those who are as hurt and disappointed as you, are hiding your status updates because they find them negative or draining. You also may want to stay away from clubs if your goal is to meet a man because you wouldn't recognize him if he had your name tattooed in neon lights all over his body. You've witnessed and/or experience so much hurt that it's hard to see anyone new without being reminded of a painful past.

I am so, so sorry for what you went through. Still, your past does not have to equal your future. Take a much-needed respite to identify your issues, work through them and emerge healthier and happier for the journey.

As you can see, the lower the score, the less identified "ish" or issues in relationships, self-worth, and attitudes towards self you may need to examine. However, wherever you fall along the scale, you picked up this book for a reason. Hence, taking a sex-free sabbatical may be perfect in helping you realize what the perfect relationship for you looks like. Notice I said *for you* because not everyone has the same needs in a relationship. Adopting a sex-free approach can also be a great way for you eliminate the clutter. In other words, use this time to identify any possible issues or hang ups you have about the opposite sex, dating, intimacy, and relationships.

For example, if you answered that sex is not one of God's greatest gifts to mankind, you may need some time to distance yourself from lackluster and underwhelming experiences in the past, so that you can have some pretty terrific mind-bending and spiritually altering sexual experiences in the future. In like turn, if you don't believe that monogamy is possible or don't have any nearby models of what a loving, committed marriage or relationship looks like, it will be incredibly difficult for you to recognize, let alone, have one.

Strong, healthy relationships do exist, but they probably won't for you if you've never seen one up close or were unable to view and/or ask the couple involved how they made it work.

Moreover, you can also use this time to recognize your own gifts. Maybe it's a great listening ear, the gifts of gab, and/or humor. Or, perhaps you are really kind and tend to believe the best in others, no matter what it looks like. If so, you may be tempted to harden yourself or not believe others because some people mistook your kindness for weakness. But, if you think about it, it's not really fair to diminish what makes you you because you met a few jokers who were too foolish to see what you had to offer. It also isn't very cool to deny others the opportunity to be blessed by all of your talents because of a rotten apple or two (or more). Those jokers have already negatively impacted your past. There's no way they should have any more access to your present or your future. Rather than closing your heart and staving off your gifts and talents, use this time to develop a better discernment of people, so that you will no longer cast your pearls before swine.

Recognizing Wants vs. Needs:

Men want sex. I know this, you know it, and so does everyone else. What a man needs, however, is generally less articulated and addressed. And, if you provide this need, he will adore and treasure you above all others who provide what he wants.

Are you ready to hear it? Before you answer, I must prepare you that you have to be in a great emotional and mental space to provide it. If you're not, your unresolved demons will get in the way and hamper your every attempt to provide this need for him.

In addition, before we discuss his need, it's equally important for you to recognize the difference between what we, as women, want versus what we need. Ask almost any man and he'll tell you that one of our most frequent requests of him is time. We always want more of it. We want to be a top priority in his life, and if he spends his time with us, we know he cares.

The problem comes when we keep making requests (which may soon be interpreted as nagging) and attempt to make him feel guilty for not honoring our wishes. He may have very good reasons for not spending time with us, including working to provide a better life for us, spending some time fellowshipping and hanging out with his friends (because that, too, is very important), or just retreating to his "cave," also known as spending time by himself. Then, if he does grant us the time, we may spend so much of it complaining about why it took so long to happen or wondering when it will happen again that we don't enjoy the moment.

There's also a chance that we may not even know why we're acting that way and neither does he.

The reason, however, is very simple. We, too, were focusing on a want versus a need. So, when he met the want, we got what we said we wanted, but it didn't fulfill our need. It's like craving a chocolate cake at dinnertime, and then getting mad if you're still hungry an hour later. You like cake, but you need food. Food satiates the hunger while cake addresses a want. In like turn, we crave more time with our men, but we need security. Dictionary.com defines security as follows:

- Freedom from danger, risk, etc.; safety.
- Freedom from care, anxiety and/or doubt; well-founded confidence.
- Something that secures or makes safe; protection; defense.
- Freedom from financial cares or from want.
- An assurance; guarantee.

As women, we love from the deepest part of ourselves. There's very little to nothing we won't do for someone we love. Unless, we feel that our love is appreciated, reciprocated, and is held in the highest regard, we will waver and flounder.

We may become angry and bitter. Then, hurt, disappointed, and furious that he doesn't understand (when admittedly we don't always *really* understand our emotional outbursts), we label him "*sshole." Sadly, the relationship may really begin to deteriorate from there.

Why? Well, because regarding a man as an *sshole and treating him like such directly contradicts what he *needs* in the relationship. It's not sex. As stated earlier, that's a want. Men need respect. Although Dictionary.com lists twelve definitions in usage as a noun and verb, the following three best exemplify the respect men need in relationship:

- Esteem for, or a sense of the worth or excellence of a person, a personal quality or ability, or something considered as a manifestation of a personal quality or ability.
- Deference to a right, privilege, privileged position, or someone or something considered to have certain rights or privileges; proper acceptance or courtesy; acknowledgment.
- The condition of being esteemed or honored [revered, held in high respect, to confer distinction upon].

Men need us to highly esteem and value them as "a man." Each man needs to feel like he is your king, and you would willingly do all for him, with deference, love and service. He needs to feel as if you will not only hang on his every word, but that you will also do what he asks with a kind heart and a generous spirit. Though a secure man will never ask you to give up everything for him, he would most certainly appreciate knowing that you would be *willing* to do so.

And, I get that even as you read this, your eyeballs may be rolling to the back of your head or you may be thinking that I am stuck in some prehistoric Neanderthal time warp, but I submit to you that any issue you may be having is not with what I'm saying, but whether or not the man or men who've popped into your head while you're reading this deserve this type of reverence. Maybe they didn't. Yet, that still doesn't mean that men, as a whole, don't require respect.

Additionally, it takes a woman who's very secure within herself and her relationship with her man in order to give him the honor and respect he needs. If you, in any way, doubt what I'm saying and only address his wants, i.e.: sex, you will come to a fork in the road. At some point he will need respect and honor, but if you've felt disregarded and insecure in the relationship to this point, you will not be able to address this need, and the relationship will ultimately dissolve.

Most often, we can only give what we receive. Hence, before we can supply his needs, we need to spend time respecting and honoring ourselves. Once you are confident in your unique talents and abilities, you can share yourself with a man without feeling like honoring him is somehow taking away from you. And, being the provider that nearly all men aspire to be, he will be more than willing to exalt you as a top priority in his life.

Reason #6: Enjoy Better Sex

Believe it or not, I am truly suggesting that being sex free is a way to better enjoy sex. Naturally, some of you may benefit from this more than others, namely those who

- Have been incredibly hurt or deceived by a cheating lover
- Have never had an orgasm
- Are numb
- Feel guilty because of religious beliefs or past experiences, including rape, molestation or incest

Biologically speaking, sex is used for procreation. It is also of great biological import to note that humans, dolphins, and West African chimpanzee, also known as bonobos, are the only species that engage in sex for pleasure. Thus, in addition to reproduction, our bodies are also designed to enjoy sex as recreation.

If you find that your sexual experiences have been less than fulfilling, consider using this hiatus to change that. There's a great deal of popular music today by male artists that focus on women being pleased according to a man's definition of how he's pleased. Included in this is sex without commitment, glorification of strippers, and using drugs to induce a more satisfying experience. There are also long held cultural, societal and/or religious beliefs about promiscuity and "loose women" that can compromise women from developing healthy attitudes about sex. Further, there are ideas about what sexual equality means for women, which promote her sexual liberation while conflicting with her personal and/or moral beliefs about intimacy.

Then, there's oxytocin, also known as "the love hormone," which is released in our brains when we have sex. Oxytocin bonds us to other people and facilitates a feeling of closeness with sexual partners. This is great when we are in love with the person we are sleeping with, but it can also create huge problems if the recipient of all this wonderful affection is a recreational sexual partner that we barely know, and/or who may (yikes!) be a complete jerk.

If, however, you are very clear about what sex means to you and hold true to these ideals when you indulge, you will naturally have a more positive experience. You will also have increased self-confidence because you've learned to honor your talents and have found at least one man who enjoys being with you for the pleasure of your company. Great sex, then, becomes a reward that you choose to share with someone you really care about without feeling insecure, guilty or unsafe in any way.

In addition, you can also use this time to explore what makes you sexy. You can and should wear beautiful, soft and well-fitted lingerie, not for a man, but for you -- under your work clothes, when traveling or just because --because you like the way you feel wearing it. You'll not only better understand, but you will also live, in a more confident space where sexiness is something you possess 24 hours a day.

Reason #7: Build a Forevermore

The concept of not having sex in order for men to hold us in the highest regard is not new. Most of us have heard it since we were very little girls. The reasons to be sex-free, however, may have been presented in a more harsh way, as our reputations were on the line. Perhaps "Little" Michael Jackson and the then-pubescent Jackson Five spelled it out most succinctly when they not only belted out during the chorus for *The Love You Save,* one of their very first hits, "S is for save it," but the catchy tune also make the politics of our reputations even more clear when Michael says, "Darling, take it slow; or someday, you'll be all alone."

Shame and fear of a less than savory reputation have been used for centuries to control women. Hence, they serve no motivating function here. Indeed, they are the complete antithesis of what *Sex Free* is all about. As we've been discussing throughout this chapter, becoming sex free, for however long of a time you decide, is a great way to nurture, love and support yourself. It helps you build discipline. Additionally, it's a way to spend "me" time that affirms your unique talents and gifts you have to offer to the world as well as providing you an opportunity to examine past experiences, thoughts, and beliefs that may hamper you from living your best life.

Thus, the main benefit that becoming sex free has as it relates to building a forevermore is that after you identify what you want and take time for yourself, you will not only be open to affection from any man but the man who's perfect *for you*. The one who not only sees the big and small things that make you beautiful, but also appreciates and even adores the weird idiosyncrasies that you feared no one would ever accept about you.

Then, you will freely give him the respect he needs, while he willingly provides you with the security you crave. And, through this process, you will continue to unite until two become one, and you build your own very personal forevermore that works specifically for both of you.

There are many reasons to become sex free, a great deal of which have been discussed in prior chapters. And while I personally benefitted a great deal from many of the results which accompany a sex-free lifestyle, my primary motivation can be summed up in the name belonging to my soul mate: Gladys L. Mickey.

There are many souls that we meet along our journey in life. Some believe that their soul mate is the person they marry; I believe that a soul mate is someone without whom you'd never truly enjoy life and yourself – a person who makes life worth living, your heart sing, and affirms your reason for being all in one. That person is my grandmother, Gladys Mickey.

When I was conceived in my mother's womb, the doctor gave my mother a delivery date of February 24th. The entire family was excited, and Grandma even more so, because that was her birthday. I surprised every one, though, and came a day early. My mother reasoned that it was because I wanted my own day; but Grandma and I knew it was because that gave us two additional days to celebrate.

I know that many people understand that grandmas are special. They are renowned for showering their grandkids with unconditional love and special treats. My grandma, though she did those things, was even more special because she took me into her home when I was seven and raised me as her own daughter, even though all of her children were grown, until I left for college. My parents were not together, and my mom was facing a life-threatening illness. Without giving it a second thought, Grandma sacrificed the time she could've spent enjoying her seasoned years raising me, going to parent-teacher conferences, and doing everything she could to make sure I had the best opportunities in life.

Thus, when I got the phone call in 2005 that the doctors found a spot on her lung, I was determined to do all that I could to help her. I understood that she was in her 80s by then, but I also knew that she willingly gave up a great deal to take me in, nurture, comfort and gently guide me into adulthood. Therefore, I was determined to do all that I could to help her.

I have been a believer for as long as I was conscious of the name Jesus Christ. Yet, I must admit that I didn't always live up to the tenets of Christianity. I was (and still am) a faithful tither and did (do) my best to do unto others as they do unto me, but I was, and still am, far from a "holy roller."

Prior to adopting a sex-free lifestyle, I knew, like most Christians, that sex outside of marriage, was a no no, but, quite honestly, I considered that commandment about as relevant in society today as laws banning Israelites from wearing a garment of linen mixed with wool (Lev 19:19). I didn't even know if I wanted to get married. I had a hard time finding anyone, from my childhood to life as a young adult, who was happily married.

I would also go to church regularly and hear pastors talk about how God was displeased or even worse watching His children having premarital sex with others. Yet, very few, if any of these religious teachers, offered alternatives beyond me feeling guilty. Additionally, I only remember one pastor and first lady of out many who were able to share their personal journey of being chaste with one another before marriage. And, while it was comforting to know that it was possible, the revelation that they married right out of high school did little for me. I was no longer a child but an adult. I lived in a very modern world, and I had a history of dating very attractive, and often times famous or influential, alpha men.

Hence, I had extreme difficulty trying to apply their experience to my life as a grown woman.

Grandma's illness, however, gave me immediate pause. If her sunset was approaching, I wanted her to leave this earth on her own terms and not because cancer or any other disease wanted to take her out in a way that was insidiously painful. So, motivated not by guilt or shame, but out of love, I turned to the Word. I meditated on God's promise that if I came boldly to the thrown of grace, I would obtain mercy and find grace in time of need (Heb. 4:16). I interceded on behalf of Grandma's health that the cancer, as it was determined, would be removed, that she would need no further treatment, such as radiation or chemotherapy, and that it, the cancer, would never resurface anywhere else in her body.

I also promised God that I would eliminate any activity that could potentially cause me to waver in my boldness, so that I could stand until the promise manifested. After conducting a thorough inventory, I knew that having sex outside of marriage was the one area where I was most vulnerable, so I gave it up. I was determined to be sex free for as long as I needed to be in order for Grandma to live a full, healthy, cancer-free life. I also never told Grandma or any members of my family. It was my personal plea before God.

Prior to Grandma's surgery, we prayed as a family that she had a successful surgery and full recovery. Her surgery lasted for about five to six hours. Afterwards, the doctors were unable to believe that they found the cancer so early, in stage one. (There are four stages of most cancers, with severity increasing as the number increases). Most often lung cancer isn't detected until symptoms occur (generally stage III or at worst IV) and by then it is often too late because the cancer has spread to the lymph nodes and possibly other parts of the body. Yet, the doctors told us that the cancer did not spread and that she would never get cancer in that area again. I temporarily put my career in Los Angeles on hold and moved to New York to help Grandma recover.

Though she had some major health challenges after that, she never suffered a relapse of cancer. She recovered and lived a full and happy life. In 2011, she made her transition in my arms while we were checking into the Four Seasons hotel on vacation in Las Vegas. We had just driven in from Los Angeles, and she told me that she wanted to use the restroom.

"Grandma," I said, "So do I. I just want to take you up and down the Strip, so you can see it before we check in." She nodded, smiled and took in the view.

Unfortunately, she never made it to our hotel room. She had a pulmonary embolism in the hotel lobby rest room. However, how many eighty-seven year olds do you know could say that they took their last breath while on vacation at one of the best hotels in the United States? Grandma lived each day to the fullest, including her last. And, for that I am forever grateful.

And, while this is not a book about faith, I do understand the role of faith in achieving something that you really want. My primary reason for adopting a sex-free lifestyle was motivated by love. It was not guided by a sense of guilt or fear or shame or any other factors that many people I have been exposed to use to promote abstinence.

We all have our reasons for everything. My motive in sharing my story with you is to affirm your own story, your own reason for disciplining your body in order to achieve something you potentially want more – a set goal, peace of mind, increased self-confidence and self esteem, a way to release the clutter of worn relationships and negative experiences, a deeper relationship with God, meeting and finding your ideal mate, and/or whatever else motivates you on your journey.

Your Decision, Your Way

When identifying your reason(s) for becoming sex free, it is incredibly important to associate it with a positive thing that you want, rather than a negative that you don't want. For example, if you're a guy, instead of wanting to stop meeting "crazy chicks," you may choose to focus on finding "the one." Or, if your faith is important to you, rather than focusing on feelings of shame that can be associated with sex outside of marriage, focus on the promises and blessings that God offers to those who are faithful and obedient.

In addition, it may also be a really great idea to formalize your commitment. While it can be something as simple as a promise you make to yourself (and/or God), it can also be tangible – something you can hold, touch and/or view that can keep you motivated in sunny and dark days alike. Three physical ways to mark your commitment include a certificate, contract and/or collage.

Certificate

If you're interested, you can enlarge and make a photocopy of the certificate included in the appendix. You can list your name, reason(s) for becoming sex free, and indicate the duration for how long you want to do it. You can then sign the document as a promise to yourself. The benefit of choosing a certificate is that it naturally affirms the positives for why you are committing to a sex-free journey.

Contract

Perhaps you are of a more formal countenance, and you need something in writing. In this instance, a contract, which like the certificate states your name, reason(s), and duration, may make more sense to you. If interested, please see a sample contract by turning to the appendix, and adapt/adjust as you see fit.

Collage

Another option, particularly for those of you who are visually stimulated and/or artistic, is to create a collage. The two most important things to include are images representing your reasons for becoming sex free and what your life will look like after you succeed.

You will need a large poster board, stick glue, a marker, and at least 10 different magazines. Use a timer (a kitchen timer or the one on your smart phone will do) to give yourself an hour – and over that time pull pictures out of the magazines that resemble your reason(s) for becoming sex free and/or how you envision your life will look once your goal is attained. Don't think; just clip.

Afterwards choose the images that you find to best represent your purpose and aspirations and paste them onto your collage. You can use a marker, if you'd like to write words to inspire, motivate and remind you why you are making this promise to yourself.

After you've made the initial decision to become sex free, the very next question is generally, "How on earth do I do it?"

After all, there aren't any hard and fast rules. For those who adhere to a particular faith, their religion may tell them to not do it, but it rarely to never offers a "how-to" manual for interacting with the opposite sex prior to marriage.

If you read magazine articles, you're also out of luck. Glossies are often loaded with information about the right time to have sex, ways to wow the object of your desire, an/or even how to handle non-committal sex in a post-monogamous world, but chances are you'll come up nil to never, never land if you're seeking advice on dating without "giving up the skins."

Admittedly, there were times when I personally considered avoiding the opposite sex altogether. I reasoned that if I threw myself into my job or a career-related task that I would be so busy that I wouldn't have time to think about the fact that I wasn't getting any.

And, it worked for a little while. But, it was a mere band-aid, not a solution. I mean, I could get all jazzed about meeting a writing deadline and want to go out to celebrate. Then, I'd realize that I didn't have anyone to celebrate with. Or, my phone would ring and I'd find myself disappointed, no matter who it was, because I yearned to hear a deep bass on the other end inquiring about my day and wondering how I was doing.

There were also those moments where I'd work myself silly in the hopes of passing out quickly, so I wouldn't have to lie in my bed jonesing over why there wasn't anyone on the other side of it to keep me warm, provide comfort, or just be there.

In those instances, I'd often remind myself of a prior relationship and how it ended. These trips down memory lane gave me a very clearly understanding of why the past should stay in the past. They also helped solidify my decision that I had no interest in any more short-term relationships. I became very clear that I wanted my next relationship to be with someone who was in it for the long haul.

Months passed by this way, when I was in my head about what I wanted, while my heart felt dogged by loneliness and isolation. Heaven forbid the person who slighted me, accidentally or not, while I was driving, at work, or even at the grocery checkout line, for they were surely subject to a lashing of my frustration and fury. It was so not a pretty picture.

Hence, I had no choice but to review my strategies of maintaining a sex-free lifestyle. For such I was rewarded with the stark reality that I didn't have any. Sure, I wasn't having sex, and, yeah, I also wasn't getting "hurt" by some guy, but I also wasn't having a great deal of fun either.

I am a people person who loves life and loves interacting with others. Yet, I found myself doing everything to retreat from the world in order to stay true to a promise I made to myself that seemed more and more impossible to realistically keep in our modern world.

Somehow my thoughts drifted to Sam Malone, the character Ted Danson played in the classic sitcom *Cheers.* The fog started lifting as it dawned on me that one of the things that made Sam so cool, in addition to his effortless looks, humorous wit, and caring but laid-back attitude, was the fact that he was a former alcoholic who chose to run a bar.

Hmmm… I wondered. Maybe there's something to that. And, granted, I realize that I'm talking about a fictional character inhabiting a imaginary world, but the core dynamic that Sam Malone faced in confronting head-on a world that scared him by not only living, but also thriving in it seemed like a paradigm worth exploring.

Maybe the solution did not lie in running away from life, but in embracing it, limitations and all.

I decided to get back out into the dating world, as scary as it was. I feared failing. I don't know about you, but I'm one of those people who is adamant about keeping her word. I grew up in Harlem, an area where people may not have a great deal of money, but they have enormous pride in intangibles, like pride, honor, and the value of one's word. My grandma, for example, focused heavily on honesty. To her, it

71

didn't matter how much money a person had. She'd often talked about how the wealthiest people were often the poorest ones in the world, particularly if they lied, cheated or stole to get what they had. "You have nothing, if you don't have your word," Grandma often said.

Grandma's theories on honesty were reinforced outside my home, as well. Whenever I played in the park, walked down the street or caught street ballers playing a pick-up basketball game, I'd often overhear Harlemites saying, in some form or fashion, "Your word is your bond." And, yeah, there was crime in my community, as statistics no doubt reflect. But, there was also a very strong sense of "honor among thieves." Keeping one's word is central to achieving this honor, thus making it an essential ethos that I've carried into my adult life.

Hence, I sat down and came up with some tips for dating sex free. Admittedly, some were born from an immediate brainstorm of how not to give it up and others happened as a result of trial and error.

If you're the type, who likes it sweet and succinct (ahem… like most guys who want solutions, not long treatises or discussions), my strategy can be summarized as follows:

1. Know your strengths and limitations
2. Don't put yourself in a situation you can't handle.

But, if you're like me, one of those people who likes to test limits just to see how far you can (potentially) push it without (hopefully) going too far, keep reading. Fellas, I must warn you that I'm speaking primarily to the ladies here because we have a tendency to want details on how-tos. Thus, continue reading at your own risk.

Some of these tips may sound comical, a few even hare-brained, but I promise you: they work. They key is finding which ones work best for you.

Tip #1: Keep it to Yourself

Don't tell a person you've just started dating that you're sex free. For starters, it's none of his/her business. It's your business. Your choice to become sex free may guide your interactions, but it doesn't have to guide your dates. Secondly, there's little to nothing to be gained from such a revelation. Unless you hate dating and have no desire to even interact with someone who's not willing to get married after the two of you say "hi," there's very little to gain from telling someone that you're on a first, second or even third date with that you've made a pact not to have sex. Not only is he/she stunned; he/she may be seriously impeded from the important work of getting to know you better because of the pink elephant you've paraded into the room.

Whether your date applauds your decision or not, this one act of admission immediately shifts the preliminary topic of getting to know one another to you being defined by a

73

singular decision. You are more than your sex life. Let the other person get the chance to know you before receiving any information that is only going to make him/her focus on only one part of you. Besides, everyone likes a little mystery when meeting someone new. Allow them that much.

Granted, you may not want to date just to date. You may also be so tired of the dating game that you'd rather chew glass than walk a few moments down the road of a budding relationship only to have everything end when the sex talk finally happens. Or, perhaps you are only interested in dating the one for you and/or someone who is already sex free and feel that the quickest way to find him is to be upfront with your sex-free lifestyle. If any of these scenarios best describe you, then certainly keeping it to yourself may be the last thing on your mind.

Case in point: I have a colleague, Nichole, who made a decision at a very young age that she was not having sex before marriage. At 30, she was contentedly single. A woman of faith, Nichole knew that a healthy, loving and committed marital union was God's perfect plan for her life, so she was neither anxious nor hurried to tie the knot, just to say that she was married. She wanted God's divinely appointed one for her. Therefore, Nichole had no problem telling a guy when the menus were still being passed during a first date that she was not sexually active. By her own admission, Nichole didn't have a lot of second dates. This, however, suited her fine.

One time she met a guy who, rather than running, found himself challenged by her open and unapologetic admission. Three years later, they were married.

I love sharing that story because it affirms that regardless of where you are and what you doing, everyone has his or her perfect match. I also realized that when I began my journey, I wasn't quite sold on marriage. I also deeply enjoy being around men. The smell, the very thought of them, fills me with such joy and lightness that I realized going out was more than about finding the right husband, it was also about having a lot of fun. And if that's your paradigm, trust me: keeping it to yourself is rock solid instruction.

Unfortunately, there was one time I failed to take my own advice. A few years ago, I ran into an ex from college. Though he no longer played college basketball and had even retired from a professional career, he still walked with the indomitable swagger of a man used to running the court.

He was also very remorseful about his behavior when we dated. He told me that he was really young, immature, and didn't know the difference between a quality woman and one who wasn't. Adding that he had just gotten out of a painful divorce, he made it very clear that he was interested in getting to know the woman that I had become, and that he had also learned enough about life and women not to force anything.

I was all in – hook, line and sinker. He invited me to Easter service. Later that week, he took me to Home Depot to help me find the right color paint for my living room. We planned when he'd help me paint while sharing a few glasses of wine. I felt so safe that the word vomit came out before I intended.

"I'm so happy we reconnected," I gushed.

"Me too," he said.

I looked into his rich, chocolate eyes and found myself unable to see straight. "I must confess. I don't plan on having sex anytime soon."

"Really?"

"I'm sorry, if that makes you upset. It's just something I'm going through right now, for me."

He looked at me, with a half smile and lifted me up. "Wow," he said as he engulfed me in a deep embrace. "Monique, I really respect that."

He kissed me passionately. When he broke away, I wanted nothing more than to draw him back in.

He kissed me lightly on the top of my forehead and said goodnight.

A few weeks passed. I hadn't heard from him, so I called. He was golfing. Then, he was on a business trip. Finally, he told me that he wasn't looking for anything serious, but he was looking to have sex. And, if I wasn't having it, he didn't want to waste my time.

Some may say that it's better that he revealed himself early. And, yeah, it was great that I got an opportunity to know who he was, but that was a very painful experience. Getting rejected doesn't feel good. For weeks, I doubted my decision, and myself, even though his behavior reinforced that I had made a good one.

The point is that I would've learned his motives without my sex-free revelation in a way where it would've been my decision to leave. Not his call to dump me because I wasn't doing something he wanted us to do. Not keeping it to myself put him in the driver's seat, a place where he didn't deserve to be. If, indeed, being sex free is about you empowering yourself, I highly encourage you to take every precaution needed to protect your heart and your emotions, especially when they may be particularly fragile.

Tip #2: Avoid Scheduling Any Encounter After 6pm

I know, I know, I could've just said, "Don't have a date after 6pm," but in our modern, non-committal age, people rarely "date." I mean you can actually be sleeping with someone and he still not consider the two of you dating. He might tell others, for example, if he talks about you at all, that you're "kicking it" or "spending some time" with one another.

Hence, I've chosen the word "encounter." And, when you encounter a member of the opposite sex who you like, try to do so before dark. And, no, I'm not saying that you can't control yourself; I am suggesting, however, that the opportunity to "slip" greatly increases at nighttime.

When you spend time with someone and it's late at night, your body has urges, and with the lack of other things to occupy it, many of us give in. There's only so much talking or movie watching you can do, before the allure of low lights, warm bodies and the inclination to cuddle, fall asleep in his arms, and potentially do other things beckons.

With that in mind, I highly urge you to make use of…

Tip #3: Make Breakfast Meetings, Lunches and Coffee Dates Your New Best Friends

Suggest breakfast, for example, before you go to work during the weekday, run errands on a Saturday, attend church and/or watch football on Sundays. In addition to keeping you out of potential trouble, breakfasts are great because they are generally affordable, perfect opportunities to have conversations and allow you an entire day to spend time with someone if things go really well.

Lunches and coffee dates fall into a similar category. When you first start connecting with someone, it's very important to see if you are compatible. If you go to the movies, you won't get a sense of whom the other person is because you aren't even talking to one another. You have no way of gauging similar interests, values, and/or anything else that shows that you two may have a great deal in common. If you go out to dinner, and happen to find out that you really like one another and want to spend more time together, how many options do you have besides going home?

I guess you can go out for additional drinks or maybe for late night coffee, but in the end, there's still only one place left to go: home. Eliminate the pressure. Schedule encounters earlier that allow you to spend more quality time with one another with a cost efficient price tag and in a less sexually charged atmosphere.

Tip #4: If you find yourself out past 7pm, schedule "An Out"

I know, by now, you won't plan on hanging out anytime after 6pm and you'll only do breakfasts and lunches, but you know what they say about the best-laid plans...

For example, there have been times when I tried to schedule an early encounter, but the guy I was interested in couldn't do it. Or we may have connected earlier, and we were having so much fun that the time melted before us, and the next thing we knew it was evening or night, we were still out, and pheromones were popping. In those instances, I've learned to schedule "an out."

Potential Out A: Plan to meet up afterwards with a close friend

Plan to do something later, such as going out for coffee, ice cream or the like with a close friend. Be sure to choose a friend, however, who will have a tizzy if you flaked on her.

Do not make plans with someone who'll let you off the hook easily for cancelling, or, even worse, cheer you entering "the danger zone."

Potential Out B: Back Up Phone Call

Another way to have an out is to have someone call you when you should be on your way home. Again, make sure that this is somebody who will hold you accountable.

Potential Out C: Ring the Alarm

A final suggestion is to set your cell phone's alarm to go off. And when it goes off, honor it and leave.

If you'd like, you can tell the person you're hanging with that you have something to do at a specific time. I wouldn't tell him exactly why you're leaving because that could open up a can of worms. At this stage, the most important information you need to reveal is that you have other plans. When that alarm goes off, both you and the person you're with knows that it means that you have other plans. Honor the alarm: Don't cancel or shut it off, especially if you know it may lead to greater temptation.

Tip #5: If You Find Yourself Out Past 10 pm, Set Up Obstacles
Again, no judgment. Some of us are more adventurous regarding our limits (i.e.: have harder heads), so in the event that you find yourself still out and about after 10pm with an object of your desire: set up obstacles.

Remember, your mother's insistence on you leaving the house with clean underwear? Well, by all means make sure they're clean. But, please also be sure that they are presentable to no one but yourself. Wear those drawers (and, yes, I mean drawers) that you reserve for that one week out of the month where our lives are turned upside down.

Yup, you got it. Wear your "period panties." Don't wear grandma briefs or spanx or anything else that may look awkward, but that he'd willingly look over for a moment of passion. Wear something that you'd prefer to die of embarrassment in on the spot, rather for him to ever see you in this particular way.

In fairness, I have a few friends who swear not by "period panties," but by going Amazon (i.e.: not shaving, waxing, or grooming their pubic areas in any way). This may not work for everyone. I, for one, feel that being well groomed makes me feel more confident. I am also not a huge fan of being negligent towards myself in anyway just to avoid having sex. But, if you can go Amazon without losing your swag, do it. If not, toss the Amazonian approach in favor of something else.

Tip #6: Know His Code

When women get together, especially the single ones, we love to pontificate about "what's wrong with him." We act completely baffled over his behavior and go to our friends to "interpret" what a particular guy we're seeing meant by what he either did or did not say or do. But, if most of us are honest, we know that it's not that we don't understand why he's acting the way he is, because he probably has told us at some earlier time, it's either a) we don't like it; b) we choose not to believe someone could really think that way; and/or c) we want to change the way he thinks, believes and/or acts.

It's our failure to accept him, or his "moral code," as is that really gets our goat. He may tell us that he's never interested in getting married or even settling down into a monogamous relationship, and instead of checking him off as a suitable mate, we want to understand why he thinks that way and, in the best of all circumstances, change him into someone who not only accepts monogamy, but will become its ring leader.

Truthfully, it's not fair. It's also not helpful... to anyone. It's not helpful to him because we're not accepting him at face value, so he'll never measure up to the man we may desire him to be in our imagination. And, it's certainly not helpful for us. Not only do we, if we're really honest, have a lot of "work" to do on ourselves, we'll never get the relationship we want because we're chasing someone with incompatible interests.

One of the benefits of being sex free is that it prevents us from hopping into bed too soon, which may emotionally cloud our vision, and give us some time to see this guy for who he is. He may actually be a great guy who's looking to settle down and have a family, but he's witnessed so many horror stories from friends, family and/or even his own parents that he plans to stay as far away from "the fire," or commitment, as possible.

If we sleep with him too fast, our intention may slip from getting to know him better to making sure he's not seeing or sleeping with anyone else. Our possessiveness may, in turn, turn him away and we're left thinking that he's another jerk, while he's simultaneously convinced that there aren't any good women left.

Conversely, if he is a midnight marauder, who's just in it to "win it," chances are he'll be very upfront about it. He will tell you how the two of you can have a lot of fun together and do his best to persuade you with a pitch about how pleasurable it will be. To him, sex may be about as personal as going to the gym and lifting weights. For you, it may be more. If you have sex with him for any reason except the fact that you want a physical release as well, you are both entering into a social contract under the guise of deception and setting yourself up for heartache. Little to no good can result from this.

Yet, all is not lost. If a man tells you what he wants, you don't have to go along. You can tell him that you respect his decision and you hope that one day you can be friends, but that you have other interests. After that, leave him alone. Move on. Don't fixate on changing him. There are so many other men who want families, yes, there truly are, that you don't have to convince someone to want what you want.

Because if you listen to a lot of men, they'll tell you that it's not that they don't want a specific woman, it's that she doesn't want what he wants or the "timing is off," which means that when she wanted a relationship, he did not. Or when he wanted one, she was no longer available.

Timing is a big word for men. They use it a lot. Instead of fighting them about "making the right time," accept their definition. There are a lot more men that the statistics may have you believe. Don't short change yourself. The timing may be off with him, but it doesn't mean that it isn't on somewhere else, with a man who is even more desirable because he wants you.

And, don't be surprised when that same man who tells you the "timing is off," sticks his head back in your direction to see if you're still available, because he just may. Again, a man, particularly an alpha male, will be the first to tell you that they like to hunt. But, in our society, there's not a lot of hunting going on because so many women fear dwindling percentages that they go after a man without allowing him the opportunity to pursue them.

And, yes, you're right, many of these men don't seem to mind these women coming after them, but when they are interested in a wife, the rules change. At this point, they will come after you.

Believe it or not, men are human. They seek connection -- the same as we do. And, like us, they may also resist if they feel forced.

Hence, knowing his code means both understanding what he's looking for and respecting it. It does not mean accepting less than you deserve, just to spend time with him. Stop competing for scraps. If you don't, you are very likely to drift into an insecure place. And insecurity reeks of desperation, which is a scent that will drive any and every man away.

So, accept his code. Be kind to him. Gently explain that you're interested in more and then let him go. Don't call him. Don't chase him. Don't wish harmful things on him because he doesn't see relationships the way you do. Let go.

If every other woman is clawing at him by 1) not accepting his code; and 2) not being honest with him in a kind and gentle way about what she really wants, you may point the way to his true north. Though you're not doing it to get him, chances are very likely that he may check back in, just to see what you're really talking about. Maybe then, the two of you can have an opportunity to really grasp and appreciate one another, which is the basis for any good thing to come.

Tip #7: Know Yourself

Before, while, and after you try all external markers to reduce the possibility that you'll have sex, know your vulnerable parts. Know when you're likely to fall and prepare yourself.

And, while honesty with yourself is clearly a driving force in practicing this tip, it is equally important that you don't judge yourself. As human beings, we are all subject to incredible acts of courage, bravery, discipline and self-sacrifice, but also quite capable of horribly missing the mark.

Choosing to become sex free, for however long you desire, does not mean that your body won't have cravings; in fact, you should expect that it will. The preceding tips are designed to help you through the temptations when, not if, they arrive, because they surely will. Even if you didn't enjoy sex very much, chances are the moment that you decide that you are consciously not going to have it, your body will wake you up in the middle of the night with night sweats or out of an orgasmic dream, to tell you that it wants to get laid.

Hence, the most important thing, is not preparing for the fall, it is to *truly* know yourself.

THE SEX FREE **RELATIONSHIP**

A sex-free relationship can be an incredibly fun, rich, and rewarding journey provided that both parties in the relationship adhere to a few guidelines. But before we delve further into these building blocks, let's do a roll call of a several well-known couples that were sex free prior to marriage:

- Angela Bassett and husband Courtney Vance
- Reverend Run and wife Justine Simmons
- *Victoria Secret's* supermodel Adriana Lima and husband Marko Jaric
- *Friend's* star Lisa Kudrow and husband Michel Stern
- Former *Los Angeles Laker* A.C. Green and wife Veronique Green
- Mariah Carey and husband Nick Cannon

Granted, Mariah and Nick married only after two months of dating. Yet, waiting, no matter how long, as some of you may now realize, is a strong test of endurance. Mariah also stands out as someone who was famously married to a high profile music exec before a very public divorce saw her reeling through her fair share of hook ups with well-known figures like baseball heartthrob Derek Jeter and rapper Eminem. Yet, when Ms. Carey was ready to settle down, she did not look at the world nor focus on what anyone else may have thought about her, her prior relationship history, and/or her decision to become sex free. Rather, she concentrated on finding someone – of like mind and purpose— who was as equally committed to a sex-free courtship.

Thus, again, I take the time to remind you that this is your choice. It doesn't matter what you've done before or how people may perceive you. Your commitment to yourself, your reason(s) for adopting a sex-free lifestyle, and your decision to share the experience with a willing partner are all that matter.

Reverend Run, wife Justine, Angela Bassett and husband Courtney Vance were also in long-term relationships with other people for years before finding one another. Reverend Run was going through a painful divorce when he re-connected with Justine, his teenage sweetheart. Although his professional career as part of the iconic group Run-DMC was riding high, he admits that had made a mess of his personal life. He promised God that if given another chance, he would do it differently. So, he was very committed to being sex free before he and Justine tied the knot. Their commitment to waiting and building a strong relationship has led to a rock-solid marriage and healthy family, as profiled on *Run's House*, which was one of MTV's most highly rated and successful reality television shows during the early 2000s.

Angela Bassett and Courtney Vance, both graduates of Yale University's School of Drama, traveled in the same circles for many years. Not only were they friends, but they also knew each other's prior live-in sweethearts. As recounted in their autobiography, *Friends: A Love* Story, Angela states that when she and Courtney reconnected, several years after both of their other relationships ended, she was committed to being sex free, but was nervous about how it might affect her potential relationship with Courtney. Her fears were quickly put to rest after he shared that like her, he had resolved, as a result of his own journey, to take a sex-free hiatus. Their decision to both become sex free, without ever knowing the other was doing it, served as a confirmation that they were on the right track. Twelve months later, they married.

In addition, as much as our modern world thinks it's impossible, there are those who were not only sex free, but also virgins on their wedding night. Adriana Lima, frequently listed as one of FHM magazine's 100 sexiest women, was a twenty-seven year old virgin when she married her husband. Prior to that, she dated rock heartthrob Lenny Kravitz and Derek Jeter.

Further, even though she was a successful actress with lots of exposure to all kinds of hot men, Lisa Kudrow maintained her purity until she married at age 32.

Former *Los Angeles Laker* A.C. Green, nicknamed "Iron Man," for playing the most consecutive games over his career, or 1278 out of 1281 games, remained a virgin in a world oversaturated with sexual opportunities, escapades, and infidelities. Yet, with all his access, A.C. did not have sex until he married two years after he retired from the NBA.

So, rest assured. If there are any among you who are still on the fence about whether they can actually find a partner who will willingly commit to a sex-free relationship, the answer is yes.

Making the Sex-Free Relationship Work

Ask anyone who has ever been in a successful relationship what made it work and you'll find trust, communication, respect, laughter, and forgiveness at the top of their lists. In like turn, fruitful unions work because both partners consciously commit to the relationship, in word and deed, and do whatever it takes to keep the warm fires burning.

Rewarding sex-free relationships work in much the same way. The decision to not have sex, however, may present some sensitivity, particularly early on in the relationship as the couple is deciding and defining what works best for them. If you and your partner are in this particular space, consider the following building blocks for lasting sex-free relationships:

Building Block #1: Both Parties Must Agree to a Sex-Free Lifestyle

This should be so automatic that it need not be mentioned. Yet, sadly, this most basic guideline is one of the most frequently overlooked. You cannot trick, harangue, or guilt anyone into doing what you are doing. You also cannot lie and pretend to be sex free, in an attempt to appease your partner. Not only are these actions disingenuous, they are serious signals that your relationship has larger issues, such as a lack of trust, fidelity, and mutual respect for one another's beliefs. You can find a partner you are attracted to who will willingly become sex free with you.

Additionally, it is extremely unwise to try and force someone to become sex free, even if you believe it's good for them. Tammy, a friend from college, was in a long-term relationship for nearly three years when her boyfriend Scott decided that they should become sex free. He and Tammy had fallen into a pattern of breaking up after some type of emotional blow out and reconnecting a short time later. The problem is that they never resolved their issues, so Scott felt that if they stopped running from their problems, which included covering their issues by having sex, they could see if they had a chance to become life partners.

Scott told Tammy that this decision was for their own good. Nearly a year later, he felt that they were in a better place and wanted to start having sex again. Not only did Tammy refuse, she also broke up with him for what she perceived as controlling and manipulative behavior.

Building Block #2: Have an End Game in Mind

Just as very few of us would get in a car or hop on a plane without a) knowing where we were going and b) knowing how long we will stay after we arrive, it's very ill advised to have two people who are physically attracted to one another and love each other deeply decide to be sex free without an end date in mind. For some people, it could be a period of time that will allow both parties to get a true idea for where the relationship is heading. For others, it could be after one of the parties achieves some goal that will allow him/her to have more time to focus on the relationship. For still others, it could be marriage. Whatever the terms, be sure that they are specific to what will work best for the relationship and the individuals involved.

Building Block #3: Be Accountable

Find someone or something that you, as a couple, can be accountable to. While there are some among us who are so disciplined that we don't need anyone outside of our own conscience to keep us on track, there are others of us who benefit greatly from having a mentor or coach, of sorts, to keep us on track. Much like individuals have personal trainers to keep them in shape and teams use coaches to help them maximize their strengths to win in their chosen field, find someone you really respect that you can share your successes and confess your areas of improvement so that you may stay on the path.

For example, is there a couple that has been sex free and is willing to share how they made it work? Do you know any happily, married couples willing to provide a listening ear and/or go out with you so that you greatly reduce opportunities to backslide or fall?

Please note: accountability may find you. More specifically, as you embark on a sex-free relationship and others find out about it, you may spark some intrigue among friends, colleagues and family members. Without using you as a "poster couple," they may take an interest in helping you complete your goal simply because they know that your decision is unique and special. Nichole and George, referenced in prior chapters, for instance, soon found George's entire apartment building, in addition to family, friends and church members, rooting them towards their goal of consummating their love on their wedding night. After they began dating, church members were very proud of the pair. They began telling others that it could be done, culminating with Nichole and George appearing on KJLH, a popular adult contemporary radio station in Los Angeles, where they discussed their desire to wait until their wedding night.

Upwards of 900,000 Angelinos tune into KJLH weekly, including, it turns out, nearly everyone in George's apartment building. Hence, Nichole often laughs when she recounts how George's neighbors would often wave when she was leaving his apartment in the evening, taking special note that there may have been a few times when they were concerned that she was leaving a "little" late.

A Final Caveat:

From personal experience, I have found that these relationships work best when the man thinks it's "his idea." Using traditional relationships as a model, men often like to lead and believe that women will follow. It doesn't matter how the conversation started or who was sex free "first."

So ladies, if you were sex free when he met you, and at some point he became open to experiencing it, know that by the time you move from dating to relationship stage, the transition may be smoother if you allow him to take the lead once you are in an actual relationship. He may, for example, have a few rules of his own that he'd like the two of you to follow. For instance, say you like petting, but he's concerned that indulging in that may cause him to "fall." Instead of resisting, respect his boundary. From there, the two of you can decide to explore alternate ways to express affection.

In like turn, gentlemen, don't be surprised if you have a harder time than you may expect for you and your partner to mutually agree on a sex-free relationship. As stated in "The Single Guy," it may take your lady to be some time to really believe that you are for real and are not just playing some type of head game by saying you want to be sex free with her, while you are getting your snatch on with somebody else.

Be patient. If she's open and the potential relationship is worth it, your understanding will most definitely pay off.

Maintaining Intimacy

Successful sex-free relationships are essentially the same as every other committed, monogamous relationship between two people who are physically attracted to and care about one another except for one caveat: there is no sexual penetration involved. This does not mean, however, that there isn't any affection. The level and type of affection expressed varies depending on the couple: how comfortable they are expressing non-sexual intimacy with one another, and their sensitivity towards expressing their love and affection for one another without "falling off the wagon."

Some couples, for example, are content with hugging. Others find kissing can become too intense, especially if they are by themselves. Yet, they like kissing and hugging, so they may do so in a public setting where their petting can't go too far. For still others, public displays of affection are absolute no no's. Every couple's journey is different, so it's best to talk to your partner about what you both are comfortable with and setting your own guidelines from there.

Suggestions for enhancing intimacy:

- Dance together
- Laugh
- Kiss
- Hug
- Hold hands
- Cook
- Read to each other
- Garden together
- Create a 5, 10, and/or 20 year "take over the world together" plan and make steps towards executing it
- Have a "Question of the Day" to ask one another

- Plant and garden together (If you're planting fruits and veggies, be sure to cook together as well)
- Ride rollercoasters and other thrill seeking rides together
- Make a cd/iTunes playlist of songs that would make a great soundtrack for your relationship
- Exercise – workout at gym, go running, walking, play basketball
- Meditate
- Pray
- Take long drives together
- Go to church together
- Create a "bucket list" and do the activities together
- Place phone calls right before you go to sleep at night and right as you wake up in the morning
- Give each other foot massages and pedicures (no polish required for the gentlemen)
- Sit and/or go for walks in the park together
- Plan an outdoor meal at the park, lake or beach (depending on location)

Women:

- Rub your beau's head
- Leave him little notes of encouragement in unexpected places

Men:

- Paint her toe nails

- Write her poetry
- Write her notes and letters sharing how much she means to you.

Is it possible to be in a long-term, monogamous relationship without having sex?

Absolutely… as long as both partners agree to it. The key: it must be mutually agreed upon. It helps if both are abstaining for reasons that will enhance both their lives as a couple and on an individual basis. Becoming sex-free should never be "sprung" on a partner without him/her having any say in the matter; nor should it be used as a method of punishment. If you do either, expect a backlash, and rightfully so. No one likes to feel that his/her choice in anything is being taken away.

And, granted, while a majority of men and women can't imagine being in a relationship with anyone they aren't having sex with, remember you don't need anyone; just the one for you.

Sex is easy. The real challenge in relationships is finding someone you deeply connect with and are incredibly passionate about, who will go to hades and back for you, without you feeling that they are trying to lay a guilt trip on you or have any other motive for helping you, sans your growth and success.

Moreover, if you're a woman in a relationship with a man, please realize that his greatest need is not sex. It is honor. Yes, he may crave sex, but he needs to be respected, embraced and treated as a man you deeply believe in, cherish and admire.

Don't you want to "test drive" before you buy?

Test-driving a car can be a great deal of fun. Not only do you get the chance to bask in a new car's fresh, intoxicating smell, you also get a chance to see how it handles bumps, breaks and turns. If it rides well, it's often a slam-dunk buy for those who knew what they wanted to begin with.

Unfortunately, test drives can also result in many a car buyer leasing or purchasing a car they would've never looked at twice, leading to quite a few questionable car choices. I've had quite a few friends who've made such decisions. Without fail, a pattern emerges. First, without any prompting on my end, every last one of them explained how they would've never given the car a second chance, but when they test drove it, it wasn't as bad as they thought. Essentially, they had lowered expectations to begin with, and then when they test-drove the vehicle, they realize that it exceeded their already low preconceptions. A few even found that they really liked the car.

Then, slowly, but surely, the repeated explanations about why they got the car, combined with a growing debt for purchasing something that wasn't initially on their radar made for a remorseful buyer. Finally, most, if not all, of them began making googly eyes for a car they originally wanted and/or dreamed about before they got side-tracked by a test drive.

Sound familiar?

It should, since a similar concept applies to dating. Test driving the merchandise, i.e.: having sex before you're ready, can be scores of fun, but you want to be careful that you don't let the emotions attached to the newness of the experience lock you into something you won't want after the razzle dazzle wears thin.

Say you're a woman who's a little older and is concerned that your fertility clock is ticking away. Would you still advise someone to become sex free?

This depends on the reasons you decide to become sex free. If they are any other than honoring your faith, where you expect God to meet your needs including having a child, then perhaps you need to seriously consider the timing of when, where and how long you choose to be sex free.

Is there such a thing as "waiting too long" to have sex?

Possibly. It depends on the connection between you and your potential paramour. You may find that what you originally hoped was a burgeoning love affair is ultimately best suited to remain a friendship – distant or active.

In addition, the timing may be off. By the time you're ready to resume sexual activity, the person you wanted to have sex with may no longer be available, physically, emotionally and/or spiritually, to engage in a sexual relationship with you.

Finally, if it's meant to be, it will be. Relationships happen. Or they don't. Goals shift. Desires sometimes change. So, make peace with all possible outcomes. That way, whether you ever have sex with that person or not, you have no regrets.

What if I have a moment of weakness and give in?

If you embark on a "moment for me" or sex-free experience, you should do all you can to stay true to your goal for as long as you desire. Let's be clear: No one should set out to fail.

If, however, you have hiccups, or moments of weakness, along your path, don't give up. You decided to embark on this journey for a reason. If you fall down, get back up. And, keep getting back up for as long as it takes. Don't give up if you fail. Keep playing until you win!

What if I forget how to, um, do it?

I know that this is a question that you probably feel really bad about asking because it sounds silly to even say, but rest assured: you won't forget. And, in the oft chance that you do forget, it might be a good thing. See, sometimes distance allows us to break from things that didn't really work in the past and opens us up to new ways of communicating. Plus, provided that you relax, you may even have a much better time than before because you are focusing specifically on your current partner and are not hampered by thoughts of what any past partner may have or have not liked.

For months and months, as I was writing *Sex Free*, I kept wondering, "How on earth am I going to end it?" Then, I realized that I the bigger question was not how it ends; it is in asking, "What happens next?" And, that my lovely reader is probably best for you to decide. If you'd like to share your experiences, comments, and the like, please email me at mnmatthews@rocketmail.com

It has been my hope to aid you on your journey. Your motivation and length of time towards completion, however, is your own personal story.

I wish you love, light and success along your journey. Happy travels!

Monique

This Certificate serves to acknowledge that

[Insert Name Above]

Has Decided to Become Sex Free For

[Insert reason(s) above]

During the following period

—

[Insert Dates or time period, if known]

_____
Signature

_____
Date

SEX FREE CONTRACT

THIS AGREEMENT serves as a binding pledge that I, _____, do hereby agree to adopt a sex-free lifestyle.

IN CONSIDERATION of this undertaking, I am documenting that I am making this decision for the following reason (s).

_____

_____

_____

_____

_____

_____

_____

_____

FURTHER, I am committed to remaining Sex Free until:

_____

_____

Other terms to be observed during this time period include but are not limited to the following:

_____

_____

_____

This is the entire agreement.

Signed on this date _____ in 20_____.

Name:_____ (print)

Signature: _____

Greg Worsham,
Lifestyles Photography

Monique N. Matthews is a Los Angeles-based writer and director. She has written for multiple film studios and production companies as well as received numerous accolades including Daily Variety's "10 Writers to Watch" and Filmmaker Magazine's "25 Filmmakers to Watch." She has directed several shorts and a nationally syndicated breast cancer awareness commercial. She enjoys running, hiking and competing in triathlons. Monique can be reached at mnmatthews@rocketmail.com.

www.ingramcontent.com/pod-product-compliance
Lightning Source LLC
Chambersburg PA
CBHW061150040426
42445CB00013B/1643